DELAWARE
TRIVIA

DELAWARE TRIVIA

COMPILED BY PHIL MILFORD

Rutledge Hill Press®

Nashville, Tennessee

A Thomas Nelson Company

Published in Nashville, Tennessee, by Rutledge Hill Press®,
a Thomas Nelson company, P. O. Box 141000,
Nashville, Tennessee 37214.

Library of Congress Cataloging-in-Publication Data

Milford, Phil, 1940-
    Delaware trivia / compiled by Phil Milford.
        p. cm.
    ISBN 1-55853-780-5
    1. Delaware Miscellanea. 2. Questions and answers. I. Title.
F164.6.M54 2001
975.1—dc21   99-36038
                                                                  CIP

Printed in the United States of America

1 2 3 4 5 6 7 8 9 PHX 05 04 03 02 01

PREFACE

To many, it's a brief stop on an Amtrak train headed from the nation's capital to points north or a blur on Interstate 95 while cutting through the urban centers of megalopolis on a trip to the South.

Others see Delaware as home to the DuPont Company, the global chemical giant that has had so much influence on the state, its people, politics, and infrastructure. Still others identify it with major banks and thousands of large and small businesses incorporated here, and with the special chancery court system that resolves their disputes.

Unknown to many passersby—who see only the shining towers of urban Wilmington and the industrial sprawl flanking the city—most of Delaware is rural, with agricultural enterprises ranging from corn and soybean growing to poultry farms and food processing plants.

What's more, the second smallest state has miles of white sandy beaches for swimming and fishing, a world-class summer seaside resort, wildlife preserves, freshwater lakes, campgrounds, hiking trails, and even a colonial tall ship. And for those who cherish the change of seasons, Delaware, nestled along the Middle Atlantic coast, has early idyllic springs, bright hot tanning-friendly summers, falls with leaves aflame, and winters that often see deep powdery snows.

As the first official state, Delaware helped create the nation. Its historic sites, cultural events, urban sophistication, rural beauty, and manageable pace continue to reinforce the notion of Delaware as truly "a Small Wonder." I hope this book will both intrigue those readers fortunate enough to live in Delaware and encourage visitors to return again and again.

To
Maureen

TABLE OF CONTENTS

GEOGRAPHY

C H A P T E R O N E

Q. Delaware has how many counties?

A. Three.

———⊙⊙⊙———

Q. What three states border Delaware?

A. Pennsylvania, Maryland, and New Jersey.

———⊙⊙⊙———

Q. The river that runs through Seaford has what name?

A. Nanticoke.

———⊙⊙⊙———

Q. The western boundary between Delaware and Maryland follows what historic survey?

A. Mason-Dixon Line.

———⊙⊙⊙———

Q. What is the capital of Delaware?

A. Dover.

Q. Unlike nearby states, what economic advantage does Delaware offer to shoppers?

A. No sales tax.

———— ❧ ————

Q. Most of the city of Wilmington lies between which two rivers?

A. Brandywine and Christina.

———— ❧ ————

Q. Running the length of Delaware, from Claymont to Delmar, is what major federal highway?

A. U.S. 13.

———— ❧ ————

Q. What are the names of Delaware's counties?

A. New Castle, Kent, and Sussex.

———— ❧ ————

Q. Delaware Bay has what source?

A. Upper Delaware River.

———— ❧ ————

Q. What is Delaware's largest city?

A. Wilmington.

———— ❧ ————

Q. Across the Nanticoke River from Seaford is what town?

A. Blades.

Q. In what county are Delaware's Atlantic Ocean beaches?

A. Sussex.

———

Q. Approximately how much rainfall does Delaware receive annually?

A. Forty-five inches.

———

Q. From north to south how long is the state?

A. Ninety-six miles.

———

Q. How did the Delmarva Peninsula get its name?

A. From Delaware, Maryland, and Virginia.

———

Q. What is the name of the ocean inlet that bisects Delaware Seashore State Park?

A. Indian River.

———

Q. The Lewes-Rehoboth Canal connects what two bodies of water?

A. Roosevelt Inlet and Rehoboth Bay.

———

Q. How many states the size of Delaware would fit into Texas?

A. 130.

Q. Newark is said to be named for what English parish, former home of a seventeenth-century settler?

A. Wark.

Q. Where do passengers arriving at Lewes on the Delaware Bay ferry embark?

A. Cape May, New Jersey.

Q. To what Delaware geographical area does "MOT" refer?

A. Middletown-Odessa-Townsend.

Q. What train line runs between Seaford and Federalsburg, Maryland?

A. Maryland and Delaware Railroad.

Q. Where is Archmere Academy, a Catholic high school and former home of financier John Jacob Raskob?

A. Claymont.

Q. How many bridges cross the Chesapeake and Delaware Canal in Delaware?

A. Five.

Q. What island is in the Delaware River east of Port Penn?

A. Reedy.

Q. The background and letters on the standard-issue Delaware license plate are what colors?

A. Blue and yellow.

Q. The Woodland Ferry crosses what waterway?

A. Nanticoke River.

Q. In what year was the Lewes-Rehoboth Canal project completed?

A. 1916.

Q. Lake Como lies in the middle of what Delaware municipality?

A. Smyrna.

Q. What was Wilmington's population in 1739?

A. Six hundred.

Q. New Castle County covers how many square miles?

A. 438.

Q. What small airport is situated next to Delaware 896 north of Middletown?

A. Summit.

Q. What is the world's longest twin-span highway bridge?

A. Delaware Memorial Bridge.

———∞∞∞———

Q. The Mispillion River divides what Delaware city?

A. Milford.

———∞∞∞———

Q. Between Ocean View and Bethany Beach lies what artificial waterway?

A. Assawoman Canal.

———∞∞∞———

Q. Approximately how many miles is Wilmington from either New York City or Washington, D.C.?

A. One hundred.

———∞∞∞———

Q. At the mouth of the Saint Jones River lies what town?

A. Bowers Beach.

———∞∞∞———

Q. How far does the Cape May–Lewes Ferry travel across Delaware Bay?

A. Sixteen miles.

———∞∞∞———

Q. The state's northern boundary is described in an arc twelve miles from the center of what town?

A. New Castle.

Q. How wide is Delaware at its broadest point?

A. Thirty-five miles.

———

Q. What is the popular name of the triangular tract where Pennsylvania, Maryland, and Delaware meet north of Newark?

A. The Wedge.

———

Q. The 1751 transpeninsular east-west line across the Delaware-Maryland border was surveyed to define land claims by what two people?

A. William Penn and Lord Baltimore.

———

Q. Delaware lies between what two large bays?

A. Delaware and Chesapeake.

———

Q. At what locations are lighthouses situated on the Sussex County shore?

A. Mispillion, Cape Henlopen, and Fenwick.

———

Q. When it was first surveyed in 1826, scenic Delaware City was intended to be as big as what upriver town?

A. Philadelphia.

———

Q. Canoot the Pirate is said to have sacked what Delaware town in 1698, terrorizing the inhabitants and stealing their valuables?

A. Lewes.

Q. What volunteer fire company serves the Newport area?

A. Minquas.

———⚬⚬⚬———

Q. Which Delaware town has six parks, a drag strip, a rail line, and the honor of being called "the Little Town Too Big for One State"?

A. Delmar (on the state line).

———⚬⚬⚬———

Q. Pierre S. du Pont, who was born in Wilmington in 1870, founded what world-renowned horticultural center just north of the Delaware state line?

A. Longwood Gardens.

———⚬⚬⚬———

Q. The English navigator Henry Hudson gave what name to the Delaware River when he discovered it in 1609?

A. South River.

———⚬⚬⚬———

Q. What is the Sussex County seat?

A. Georgetown.

———⚬⚬⚬———

Q. Mount Cuba is in what county?

A. New Castle.

———⚬⚬⚬———

Q. The twin Delaware Memorial Bridges carry what two highway designations?

A. I-295 and U.S. 40.

Q. In what year did the U.S. Supreme Court rule that upper Delaware's eastern boundary extended across the Delaware River to the mean low-water line in New Jersey?

A. 1935.

Q. How many minutes does it take to cross Delaware Bay on the Cape May–Lewes Ferry?

A. Seventy.

Q. During World War II what organization patrolled the Delaware shoreline in small planes looking for enemy submarines?

A. Civil Air Patrol.

Q. Until 1792, what was the Sussex County seat?

A. Lewes.

Q. Where are the three Amtrak stations in northern Delaware?

A. Newark, Wilmington, and Claymont.

Q. In what town is Delaware's U.S. Department of Veterans Affairs Hospital?

A. Elsmere.

Q. In addition to being called the First State, Delaware has what other nickname?

A. The Diamond State.

Q. The Aetna Hose Hook and Ladder fire company serves which community?

A. Newark.

———∞———

Q. What is the seat of Kent County?

A. Dover.

———∞———

Q. In what Delaware town is the Wild Quail Country Club?

A. Wyoming.

———∞———

Q. What is the formal name of the Delaware Turnpike south of Wilmington?

A. John F. Kennedy Memorial Highway.

———∞———

Q. Seaford, the location of the DuPont Company's first nylon fiber plant in 1939, has what nickname?

A. Nylon Capital.

———∞———

Q. Frogtown Crossing is in what county?

A. New Castle.

———∞———

Q. What largely uninhabited tract of land is just north of the Port of Wilmington?

A. Cherry Island.

Q. Kent County contains how many square miles?

A. 594.

———∞———

Q. Where was the old New Castle County Correctional Institution, now memorialized by a lone watch tower?

A. Prices Corner.

———∞———

Q. Hardscrabble is in which county?

A. Sussex.

———∞———

Q. William Penn issued a warrant in 1683 to survey the site of a town to be known by what name?

A. Dover.

———∞———

Q. Wilmington's population had reached what number by 1850?

A. Thirteen thousand.

———∞———

Q. In 1651 Peter Stuyvesant, governor of the Dutch colony of New Netherland, built Fort Casimir at the site of what present-day town?

A. New Castle.

———∞———

Q. Woodland Beach is adjacent to what national wildlife refuge?

A. Bombay Hook.

Q. What is the speed limit on Delaware's unmarked two-lane rural roads?

A. Fifty-five miles per hour.

—⚬—

Q. How many highway miles is the distance from Claymont to Fenwick Island?

A. Approximately 115.

—⚬—

Q. In which Sussex County town is Beebe Hospital?

A. Lewes.

—⚬—

Q. Built in the 1950s, what was Delaware's first large shopping center?

A. Wilmington Merchandise Mart.

—⚬—

Q. Where is the Delaware National Guard's summer encampment training ground?

A. Bethany Beach.

—⚬—

Q. Wesley College and Delaware State University are in what city?

A. Dover.

—⚬—

Q. How long are the Delaware Memorial Bridges?

A. 2,150 feet.

Q. Mount Moriah is in what county?

A. Kent.

———⊱⊰———

Q. Which waterway flows through Yorklyn to Stanton?

A. Red Clay Creek.

———⊱⊰———

Q. The stately Wilmington Trust Company Building on Rodney Square was formerly the site of what structure?

A. Post Office.

———⊱⊰———

Q. White Clay Creek flows from north of Newark to which town?

A. Stanton.

———⊱⊰———

Q. What is the more common name for Wilmington's multipurpose criminal justice facility?

A. Gander Hill Prison.

———⊱⊰———

Q. What latitude runs just below Dover?

A. Thirty-nine degrees north.

———⊱⊰———

Q. In the 1960s, what was the name of New Castle County Airport?

A. Greater Wilmington Airport.

Q. Where is northern Delaware's Chinese Community Center?

A. Hockessin.

Q. Wilmington hit a peak population of 112,504 in what year?

A. 1940.

Q. Wilmington has what four foreign sister cities?

A. Watford, England; Kalmar, Sweden; San Juan, Guatemala; and Arad, Israel.

Q. What are Delaware's state colors?

A. Blue and buff.

Q. Wilmington's Federal Building was named after what U.S. senator from Delaware?

A. J. Caleb Boggs.

Q. Wilmington's Polish community is in what neighborhood?

A. Hedgeville.

Q. The Chesapeake and Delaware Canal is how many miles long?

A. Fourteen.

Q. Near which Delaware town is a Mennonite community?

A. Dover.

———◈———

Q. Mill Creek Volunteer Fire Company engines are painted what color?

A. Green.

———◈———

Q. What is Delaware's northernmost community?

A. Beaver Valley.

———◈———

Q. What structure formerly stood on the site of Wilmington's Trolley Square?

A. A streetcar and bus barn.

———◈———

Q. What is the state song?

A. "Our Delaware."

———◈———

Q. Dover is at approximately the same latitude as what Greek island?

A. Corfu.

———◈———

Q. Native Americans mined flint for arrowheads in what area near Newark?

A. Iron Hill.

Q. In Delaware what historic non-jury judicial body deals with corporate litigation?

A. Court of Chancery.

———∞∞∞———

Q. A statue near the Federal Building in Wilmington honors what early minister?

A. Peter Spencer.

———∞∞∞———

Q. What historic shipbuilding town was in Sussex County?

A. Bethel.

———∞∞∞———

Q. Where in Kent County is Delaware's geographical center?

A. Eleven miles south of Dover.

———∞∞∞———

Q. Before the Delaware Memorial Bridge was built, a ferry took cars and passengers from New Castle to what then-thriving New Jersey town?

A. Penns Grove.

———∞∞∞———

Q. Where in Sussex County is John West Park?

A. Ocean View.

———∞∞∞———

Q. In the state charter of 1891, what name was given to Rehoboth Beach?

A. Cape Henlopen City.

Q. The Kent County–Sussex County line divides which city?

A. Milford.

―――⚬⚬⚬―――

Q. The landfill area on the Delaware River south of the Wilmington Marine Terminal has what avian name?

A. Pigeon Point.

―――⚬⚬⚬―――

Q. In colonial times, the route that is now U.S. 13 (Philadelphia Pike) between Claymont and Wilmington had what name?

A. King's Highway.

―――⚬⚬⚬―――

Q. The state office building in Wilmington is named after which governor?

A. Elbert Carvel.

―――⚬⚬⚬―――

Q. From what source did seventeenth-century English explorers choose the name for Rehoboth Bay?

A. Genesis 26:22.

―――⚬⚬⚬―――

Q. Which colonial lawyer and patriot is buried on Quaker Hill, Wilmington?

A. John Dickinson.

―――⚬⚬⚬―――

Q. How many people live in the seaside town of Lewes?

A. Twenty-five hundred.

Q. Many of Delaware's Nanticoke Indians live near what Sussex County community?

A. Millsboro.

———◆◆◆———

Q. Where was Wilmington's Dravo Shipyard located?

A. Foot of South Madison Street.

———◆◆◆———

Q. Legend suggests that Edward Teach, aka Blackbeard the Pirate, gave his name to what Delaware community?

A. Blackbird.

———◆◆◆———

Q. Where is historic Packet Alley?

A. New Castle.

———◆◆◆———

Q. By how many square miles is Delaware larger than Rhode Island, the smallest state?

A. 937 (1,982 compared to 1,045).

———◆◆◆———

Q. What Smyrna mansion, started about 1684, was once the home of a president of the state, Thomas Collins?

A. Belmont Hall.

———◆◆◆———

Q. The Chesapeake and Delaware Canal bisects what Delaware town?

A. Saint Georges.

Q. What was the original name of Dagsboro?

A. Blackfoot Town.

———⊗———

Q. What longitude runs just east of Fenwick Island?

A. Seventy-five degrees west.

———⊗———

Q. What is the correct pronunciation for the town of Houston?

A. HOW-ston.

———⊗———

Q. Where does Delaware rank among the fifty states in population?

A. Forty-sixth.

———⊗———

Q. What is the only Delaware river that flows west to the Chesapeake Bay?

A. Nanticoke.

———⊗———

Q. Delaware corporations account for what percentage of the *Fortune* 500 companies?

A. Around fifty percent.

———⊗———

Q. Mermaid, on Limestone Road above Pike Creek, derived its name from what establishment?

A. A tavern.

Q. Early settlers gave what name to the Christina River?

A. Minquas Kill.

———∞———

Q. The names of what five towns end with the suffix *ford*?

A. Milford, Seaford, Brenford, Frankford, and Middleford.

———∞———

Q. Where in Lewes can visitors find the gravestone of an eighteenth-century woman born on the impossible date of Feb. 30?

A. St. Peter's Church.

———∞———

Q. What Delaware city contains "the Circle" as its center?

A. Georgetown.

———∞———

Q. Millsboro Pond covers how many acres?

A. 101.

———∞———

Q. In which town is the eighteenth-century Parson Thorne Mansion located?

A. Milford.

———∞———

Q. The rails on Delaware's earliest railroad, the New Castle and Frenchtown, were made of what material?

A. Wood.

Q. What structure originally stood where New Castle's Immanuel Church now stands?

A. A fort.

———— ∞ ————

Q. The great swamp in Sussex County has what nickname?

A. Delaware's Everglades.

———— ∞ ————

Q. What is Delaware's population density per square mile?

A. About 350.

———— ∞ ————

Q. Legend says Slaughter Beach got its name from what event?

A. The massacre of hostile Indians by colonial settlers.

———— ∞ ————

Q. What is Delaware's southernmost state park?

A. Trap Pond.

———— ∞ ————

Q. The old Adas Kodesch Synagogue was completed in 1908 at what Wilmington location?

A. Sixth and French Streets.

———— ∞ ————

Q. When it first began in 1831, what sort of locomotion drove the New Castle and Frenchtown Railroad?

A. Horses.

Q. Where in Brandywine Hundred is Blue Ball?

A. Concord Pike at Rockland Road.

———⸺———

Q. In what county does the Delaware Army National Guard keep its helicopters?

A. New Castle.

———⸺———

Q. Where does the Chesapeake and Delaware Canal join the Delaware River?

A. Reedy Point.

———⸺———

Q. Where is the restored eighteenth-century John Dickinson Plantation?

A. Just south of Dover.

———⸺———

Q. The new riverfront park on the Christina in Wilmington is named after what two heroes of the Underground Railroad?

A. Harriet Tubman and Thomas Garrett.

———⸺———

Q. What was Delaware's first capital?

A. New Castle.

———⸺———

Q. What percentage of the Delaware population lives in rural areas?

A. Twenty-seven percent.

Q. Frogtown Crossing adjoins what municipality?

A. Middletown.

Q. What was the original name of the three-thousand-acre tract upon which Laurel was built in 1802?

A. Bachelor's Delight.

Q. Wilmington Country Club traces its history to what earlier facility, opened in 1883?

A. Young America Cricket Club.

Q. Centreville, north of Wilmington, lies at what altitude above sea level?

A. 438 feet.

Q. Where was Delaware's George Read, signer of the Declaration of Independence, buried?

A. Immanuel Church, New Castle.

Q. In what city is Nanticoke Memorial Hospital?

A. Seaford.

Q. The Delaware 141 bridge over the Brandywine is named after what prominent Delawarean?

A. J. H. Tyler McConnell.

Q. What is the easternmost bridge over the Chesapeake and Delaware Canal?

A. Reedy Point.

———◦◦◦———

Q. Delaware's highest point on Ebright Road in New Castle County is how high above sea level?

A. 448 feet.

———◦◦◦———

Q. Where was the old Bellanca Field and aircraft factory?

A. Near New Castle.

———◦◦◦———

Q. In what suburban community is Wilmington Friends School located?

A. Alapocas.

———◦◦◦———

Q. Broad Dyke in Old New Castle was originally built by Dutch settlers in what year?

A. 1655.

———◦◦◦———

Q. In what year was the town of St. Georges incorporated?

A. 1825.

———◦◦◦———

Q. The Rehoboth Beach Boardwalk is how many feet long?

A. 5,280 (exactly one mile).

Q. For whom is Fox Point in the Edgemoor area named?

A. Marston Fox, community activist.

———⚬⚬⚬———

Q. What was the last toll road built in Delaware?

A. Wilmington and Kennett Turnpike.

———⚬⚬⚬———

Q. Where in Delaware is the community popularly known as "Dobbinsville"?

A. South of New Castle.

———⚬⚬⚬———

Q. Marshallton lies on what New Castle County waterway?

A. Red Clay Creek.

———⚬⚬⚬———

Q. Seaford, laid out in 1799, was earlier known by what name?

A. Hooper's Landing.

———⚬⚬⚬———

Q. In 1911 what prominent benefactor offered to build a major highway the length of the state, at his own expense?

A. T. Coleman du Pont.

———⚬⚬⚬———

Q. In what year was the first bridge built across the Brandywine at Market Street?

A. 1764.

Q. What brick plantation dwelling built in the mid-1700s is now in the Bombay Hook Wildlife Refuge?

A. Allee House.

———

Q. T. Coleman du Pont contributed how much money toward construction of his statewide highway project?

A. About $4 million.

———

Q. What was the steamboat fare from Philadelphia to Wilmington in the 1850s?

A. Thirty-eight cents.

———

Q. The housing community near Claymont that was built for workers at the old Worth Steel Company in the early 1900s now has what name?

A. Knollwood.

———

Q. When was Edgar M. Hoopes Reservoir and Dam built north of Wilmington?

A. 1929–1932.

———

Q. How long is the Brandywine River from its source to Wilmington?

A. Sixty miles.

———

Q. Factory outlet stores are situated near which Sussex County city?

A. Rehoboth Beach.

Q. Historic Odessa, originally called Appoquinimink, was later known by what other name?

A. Cantwell's Bridge.

Q. Where do historians say the New Castle County area known as Bear got its name?

A. The Bear tavern.

Q. The historic Alfred I. du Pont Nemours estate near Rockland Road covers how many acres?

A. Three hundred.

Q. In what year was the first span of the Delaware Memorial Bridge finished?

A. 1951.

Q. Camp Arrowhead is on what Sussex County waterway?

A. Rehoboth Bay.

Q. What Wilmington public building now stands on the site which, from 1805 until 1971, held historic Ezion Methodist Episcopal Church?

A. Carvel State Building.

Q. What program attempts to link the state's parks by walking trails?

A. Delaware Greenways.

Q. Before it became New Castle, the historic town six miles south of Wilmington had what name?

A. New Amstel.

———

Q. What are the three components of Delaware's interstate highway system?

A. I-95, I-295, and I-495.

———

Q. The upscale community of Westover Hills is said to have earned what nickname after the great stock market crash of 1929?

A. Leftover Bills.

———

Q. How high is Edgar M. Hoopes Reservoir and Dam?

A. 135 feet.

———

Q. The National Register of Historic Places lists what village founded in 1900 in northern Delaware?

A. Arden.

———

Q. What former military installation on Delaware 36 east of Milford was used during World War II to house German prisoners of war?

A. Fort Saulsbury.

———

Q. How many U.S. companies are incorporated in Delaware?

A. Around 300,000.

Q. Where in Sussex County is Delaware's self-proclaimed "youngest town"?

A. Dewey Beach.

Q. The Delaware Department of Transportation places cameras to monitor heavy holiday traffic flow on what objects?

A. Tethered balloons.

Q. Why do so many firms file their incorporation papers in Delaware?

A. Low fees, a favorable business climate, and friendly courts.

Q. Radio Station WDOV is located in which city in Delaware?

A. Dover.

Q. The state seal contains what seven symbols?

A. Wheat, corn, an ox, water, a ship, a farmer, and a militiaman.

Q. Where in southern Delaware can visitors see a unique log house apparently used in the mid-nineteenth century as slave quarters?

A. Governor Ross Plantation, Seaford.

Q. George Washington used what now-restored dwelling in Stanton during part of the Revolutionary War?

A. Hale-Byrnes House.

Q. On what island is historic Fort Delaware located?

A. Pea Patch.

———∞∞∞———

Q. The eclectic collection of early Wilmington houses relocated to near Fifth and Market Streets and preserved for posterity is known by what name?

A. Willingtown Square.

ENTERTAINMENT

C H A P T E R T W O

Q. What world-class reggae musician once lived in Wilmington?

A. Bob Marley.

———⊗⊗⊗———

Q. "Delaware's Little Broadway" is the nickname of which Wilmington theater?

A. The Playhouse.

———⊗⊗⊗———

Q. What movie was filmed in part at Saint Andrew's School, Middletown?

A. *Dead Poet's Society*.

———⊗⊗⊗———

Q. What Wilmington-born actress starred in the movies *Leaving Las Vegas*, *The Saint*, and *Palmetto*?

A. Elisabeth Shue.

———⊗⊗⊗———

Q. Enameled Easter eggs and a thousand other items of a 2000–01 Wilmingtons Riverfront Arts Center exhibit were the handiwork of what European jeweler?

A. Fabergé.

Q. What jazz trumpeter and recording artist grew up on Wilmington's East Side?

A. Clifford Brown.

———∞∞∞———

Q. What movie star from Delaware appeared in the film *I Know What You Did Last Summer*?

A. Ryan Phillippe.

———∞∞∞———

Q. Actor Robert Mitchum attended what Delaware high school while growing up on his grandparents' farm?

A. Felton.

———∞∞∞———

Q. Built in the 1870s, the historic building at Main and South Streets in Smyrna functioned as what type of facility?

A. Opera house.

———∞∞∞———

Q. Delaware-born actress Valerie Bertinelli grew up in which New Castle County suburb?

A. Claymont.

———∞∞∞———

Q. A fifty-minute steam-engine train ride from Lewes during the summer months is operated by what organization?

A. Queen Anne's Railroad.

———∞∞∞———

Q. A popular acrobatic trio founded what Delaware dinner theater?

A. Three Little Bakers.

Q. The Columbus Inn restaurant on Pennsylvania Avenue in Wilmington was known by what name in 1798?

A. Schmalz's Bakery.

Q. *Mode* magazine has featured what Delaware native, a TV and musical star, as a full-figured model?

A. Yvette Freeman.

Q. What is the name of the historic African-American folk festival held annually in Wilmington?

A. August Quarterly Festival.

Q. Wilmington's old Academy of Music opened in 1884 at what location?

A. Delaware Avenue and Orange Street.

Q. What portly 1960s rock legend twisted again at Rodney Square in the summer of 2000?

A. Chubby Checker.

Q. What world-class professional musical group gives its home concerts in Wilmington's Grand Opera House?

A. Delaware Symphony Orchestra.

Q. Where is Delaware's annual Apple-Scrapple Festival held?

A. Bridgeville.

Q. The massive rummage sale sponsored annually by the Junior League of Wilmington has what name?

A. Whale of a Sale.

Q. What night club spurred interest in development along Wilmington's South Madison Street?

A. The Big Kahuna.

Q. What historic vaudeville stage and movie house is still in use in Middletown?

A. Everett Theater.

Q. Every New Year's Eve, tens of thousands gather on Wilmington's Market Street for what festival?

A. First Night.

Q. What bushy-chinned tavern keeper gave the name to Kelly's Logan House in Wilmington in 1889?

A. John "Whiskers" Kelly.

Q. In what year did the Delaware lottery begin operations?

A. 1975.

Q. What magnet school in Wilmington is devoted to training entertainers?

A. Cab Calloway School of the Arts.

Q. The annual summer event in Middletown to remember a nineteenth-century orchard product has what name?

A. Olde Tyme Peach Festival.

Q. What rock 'n' roll tavern in Newark has introduced generations of students to beer and big-name bands?

A. Stone Balloon.

Q. Popular-music lyricist Joseph Cocucci of Middletown has what vocation?

A. Catholic priest.

Q. In 1931 what popular Broadway actor founded the Robin Hood Theater in Arden?

A. Edwin Ross.

Q. What is the diameter of the world's largest frying pan?

A. Ten feet.

Q. What actor from Delaware appeared with Tim Allen in the 1994 comedy *The Santa Clause*?

A. Judge Reinhold.

Q. Wilmington-born actress Valerie Bertinelli married what rock star?

A. Eddie van Halen.

Q. Actress Yvette Freeman, known for her roles in *ER* and a musical about singer Dinah Washington, was born in what city?

A. Wilmington.

Q. The Delmarva Irish Society holds what fall event to honor a patron saint?

A. Halfway to Saint Patrick's Day party.

Q. Held for more than thirty-five years, what annual fall event welcomes "treasure seekers" of all tastes?

A. Delaware Antiques Show.

Q. The Wilmington Theater Company traced its roots to the performance of what Shakespearean play in 1834?

A. *The Merchant of Venice.*

Q. When did the Delmarva Chicken Festival begin?

A. 1950.

Q. What do Wilmington officials paint on center-city streets for the annual Saint Patrick's Day parade?

A. Green lines.

Q. For three decades, what eighty-voice choral group has presented major works in area churches?

A. Northern Delaware Oratorio Society.

Q. A University of Delaware faculty quintet gives public performances in what type of music?

A. Jazz.

———⊗⊗⊗———

Q. Participants taking an annual midwinter dip in the ocean at Bethany Beach call their frigid event by what name?

A. "Exercise Like the Eskimos."

———⊗⊗⊗———

Q. What rock star from Wilmington was also a semipro baseball player?

A. George Thorogood.

———⊗⊗⊗———

Q. Delaware's Andy King, a bassist, played with what famous regional band?

A. The Hooters.

———⊗⊗⊗———

Q. What is the name of the Delaware Theatre Company's quarterly publication?

A. *Encore.*

———⊗⊗⊗———

Q. What annual ethnic festival is sponsored by first-staters of German extraction?

A. Delaware Saengerbund Oktoberfest.

———⊗⊗⊗———

Q. What was the name of George Thorogood's rock band?

A. The Delaware Destroyers.

Q. In what year did Arden thespians begin presenting Shakespeare's plays?

A. 1907.

———∞∞∞———

Q. The first operatic presentations were performed in southern Delaware in what year?

A. 1798.

———∞∞∞———

Q. The Three Little Bakers of Delaware dinner theater fame took what professional stage name in national tours in the 1930s?

A. Acromaniacs.

———∞∞∞———

Q. What song honors Delaware's largest city?

A. "Hail Wilmington."

———∞∞∞———

Q. A spoof of Philadelphia's Mummers Parade, what Middletown event has been held every New Year's Day for over a quarter century?

A. Hummers Parade.

———∞∞∞———

Q. Visitors to the annual Delmarva Chicken Festival can see a replica of what culinary centerpiece now on display at the Delaware History Museum in Wilmington?

A. World's largest frying pan.

Q. Sussex County annually holds what public post-Halloween event that draws thousands to see modern-day, cannon-like Rube Goldberg types of apparatus in action?

A. Punkin Chunkin.

───◦∞◦───

Q. The fifty-year-old railroad tavern-restaurant near the Amtrak station in Wilmington has what name?

A. Bernie's.

───◦∞◦───

Q. What TV actress seen on Comedy Central grew up in Ardentown and attended St. Mark's High School?

A. Allison Dunbar.

───◦∞◦───

Q. The annual Wild West Days Rodeo is held every June in which Delaware town?

A. Harrington.

───◦∞◦───

Q. For decades in New Castle County, what 1950s-style hamburger restaurant on Concord Pike has been a teenage favorite?

A. Charcoal Pit.

───◦∞◦───

Q. What TV actor once played for the Wilmington Blue Bombers basketball team?

A. Chuck Conners.

Q. Wilmington's August Quarterly Festival originally celebrated what annual event?

A. End of harvest.

Q. Actress Valerie Bertinelli attended what North Wilmington Roman Catholic school?

A. Holy Rosary.

Q. Where in northern Delaware is an annual Civil War reenactment held each spring?

A. Brandywine Creek State Park.

Q. Which Wilmington businessman founded Haneef's African Festival in 1985?

A. Haneef Shabazz.

Q. In what year did the first theater in the DuPont Building open?

A. 1913.

Q. In addition to Wilmington, what four Delaware towns built their own opera houses before moving film was invented?

A. New Castle, Newark, Smyrna, and Dover.

Q. What are the call letters of Delaware's public television station?

A. WHYY-TV.

Q. The grandiose 1893 structure at the corner of Wilmington's Jackson Street and Delaware Avenue houses what institution?

A. Delaware Children's Theatre.

———— ∞∞∞ ————

Q. Visitors to what Victorian suburban Wilmington estate can enjoy summer concerts of Irish, bluegrass, and folk music?

A. Rockwood Mansion.

———— ∞∞∞ ————

Q. What was the name of the luncheon tour and discussion series hosted by the Delaware Art Museum?

A. Starving for Art.

———— ∞∞∞ ————

Q. Memories of the beaches are aplenty in *The Delaware Seashore: A Photographic Journey*, a 1989 book by what photographer?

A. Michael Biggs.

———— ∞∞∞ ————

Q. Delawareans Tony Goddess and Shivika Asthana were members of what popular Boston-based music group?

A. Papas Fritas.

———— ∞∞∞ ————

Q. Sounds of swing permeate the salt air at Rehoboth Beach every fall for what event?

A. Autumn Jazz Festival.

———— ∞∞∞ ————

Q. What Wilmington church is adjacent to Rodney Square?

A. First and Central Presbyterian.

Q. What former Delawarean made television documentaries about the Civil War and baseball?

A. Ken Burns.

———⊗⊗⊙———

Q. Where has the annual Delaware State Fair been held in recent years?

A. Harrington Fairgrounds.

———⊗⊗⊙———

Q. How many hotel rooms are available for business people and tourists in the Greater Wilmington area?

A. About six thousand.

———⊗⊗⊙———

Q. Delaware native Valerie Bertinelli became a star in the 1970s in what TV series?

A. *One Day at a Time.*

———⊗⊗⊙———

Q. What was the former name of the building now home to the Delaware Children's Theatre?

A. New Century Club.

———⊗⊗⊙———

Q. Creative children and adults can get their hands dirty, carve to their hearts' content, and compete for prizes at what annual beach event?

A. Seashore Sandcastle Contest.

Q. In what month can visitors tour inns and bed-and-breakfasts at the Delaware beaches?

A. April.

———————

Q. The Riverfront Playhouse on South Walnut Street is in what Delaware town?

A. Milford.

———————

Q. What organization sponsors the annual Wilmington Christmas Parade?

A. Jaycees.

———————

Q. Saturday musical events for elementary school children at Wilmington's Grand Opera House have what name?

A. Lollipops Concerts.

———————

Q. Dover's Capitol Theater, built in 1904, originally served what function for townspeople?

A. Opera house.

———————

Q. In what year did the Logan House at Wilmington's Trolley Square begin operation?

A. 1864.

Q. Who was the beloved male ballet instructor at the Academy of the Dance who regularly performed with Delaware students in *The Nutcracker*?

A. Jamie Jamieson.

Q. What Wilmington-based affinity group is dedicated to promoting blues music?

A. Diamond State Blues Society.

Q. Newark's Bob Carpenter Center hosts what annual event featuring ideas for cooking, remodeling, and decorating?

A. Delaware Home Show.

Q. The Wilmington and Western steam railroad began excursion tours in what year?

A. 1982.

Q. In early December officials host what public singing event in central Wilmington?

A. Caroling on Rodney Square.

Q. The annual Miss Delaware pageant is held in Rehoboth Beach in what month?

A. June.

Q. Seaford's Towne and Country Fair is held at what local museum-estate?

A. Governor Ross Plantation.

Q. The historic movie theater in Smyrna, operated for many years by the Schwartz family had what name?

A. Strand.

Q. Where is the celebrated seaside watering hole the Bottle and Cork located?

A. Dewey Beach.

Q. Spurred by complaints from Quakers, Delaware outlawed public fairs in what year?

A. 1785.

Q. For twenty-five years what state group has been promoting public educational activities linking people, cultures, and ideas?

A. Delaware Humanities Forum.

Q. In what New Castle area neighborhood did film star Ryan Phillippe live as a child?

A. Penn Acres.

Q. The Grand Opera House in Wilmington was built as part of what larger structure?

A. The Masonic Hall.

Q. According to tourism officials, how many restaurants are in the Greater Wilmington area?

A. Four hundred.

Q. The annual Hispanic Festival and Puerto Rican Day Parade take place on what West Wilmington thoroughfare?

A. West Fourth Street.

Q. The annual event Dance for Plants, held near Wilmington's Trolley Square, benefits what organization?

A. Delaware Center for Horticulture.

Q. The Delaware Symphony Orchestra has been conducted by whom since the late 1970s?

A. Stephen Gunzenhauser.

Q. The 1990s television show *The Pretender* focused on what imaginary Delaware locale?

A. Blue Cove.

Q. What is the name of the state's professional opera group?

A. OperaDelaware.

Q. What is the name of the interactive, multidisciplinary, hands-on museum for youngsters in New Castle County?

A. Delaware Children's Museum.

Q. World War II B-17 pilot Ralph Minker, subject of a Delaware History Center exhibit, had what name painted on his aircraft?

A. Blue Hen Chick.

Q. Harmon R. Carey Jr. founded what group that strives to preserve Delaware's black heritage?

A. African-American Historical Society.

Q. What statewide Italian restaurant chain and tourist fixture was founded in 1960 in Rehoboth Beach?

A. Grotto Pizza.

Q. What three former University of Delaware students started the professional City Theater Company in Wilmington?

A. Tom Shade, Michael Gray, and Jon Cooper.

Q. How much did Frank Stephens and William Price pay for the 163 acres that made up the original village of Arden?

A. Nine thousand dollars.

Q. Wilmington's Playhouse Theatre contains how many seats?

A. 1,240.

Q. In 1955 what Delawarean founded the *MT Show* for teenagers?

A. Mitch Thomas.

Q. The group Sargam, founded in Newark in 1994, holds concerts and promotes the music of what country?

A. India.

Q. Wilmington's celebrated Polish Library Association is primarily known for what amenity?

A. Men's club and bar.

Q. What Methodist minister and former slave founded Wilmington's August Quarterly Festival in 1814?

A. Reverend Peter Spencer.

Q. What community theater on Lea Boulevard presents adult and children's shows?

A. Wilmington Drama League.

Q. When the Delaware Symphony Orchestra was founded in 1929, who first conducted it?

A. Harry Strausebach.

Q. What 1980s Delaware band took its name from a deck of cards?

A. Jack of Diamonds.

Q. What was the name of the outdoor movie theater near Camden?

A. Diamond State Drive-In.

Q. The Georgian-style bed-and-breakfast inn in Milford that dates to the 1600s has what name?

A. Causey Mansion.

Q. The Historic Cannonball House in Lewes is used for what purpose?

A. Marine Museum.

Q. What local custom for Wilmington African Americans gave the Monday Club its name?

A. Servants' day off.

Q. What early twentieth-century swimming area and amusement park was situated along the Delaware River at New Castle?

A. Deemer's Beach.

Q. Where in the historic Greenville area of New Castle County can music lovers enjoy pop concerts?

A. Hagley Museum.

Q. How many pipes does the theater organ in John Dickinson High School have?

A. Forty-three hundred.

Q. Pin the Tail on the Menorah is one of the games offered at the Jewish Community Center near Wilmington during what festive year-end event?

A. Chanukah Choopla.

Q. For over sixty years, Delaware's Polish-Americans have honored what Revolutionary War hero with a parade and memorial mass?

A. General Casimir Pulaski.

Q. The first exhibition in 1998 at the Christina Riverfront Arts Center in Wilmington focused on what European royal couple?

A. Nicholas and Alexandra of Russia.

Q. The Possum Point Players formed a community theater company in what city?

A. Georgetown.

Q. For more than twenty years, beginning in 1955, who conducted the Delaware Symphony Orchestra?

A. Van Lier Lanning.

Q. Native Americans from how many different tribes take part in the annual Nanticoke Pow-wow near Millsboro?

A. Fifty.

Q. What nineteenth-century orchestra became the Delaware Symphony?

A. Tankopanicum.

———

Q. The legendary Leo Ahramjian, Dana Pyle, and Frederick Gollub all played what instrument with the Delaware Symphony?

A. Violin.

———

Q. Andrew Shue, a brother of Wilmington-born actress Elisabeth Shue, was a star in what long-running television drama?

A. *Melrose Place.*

———

Q. In what month does the fishing community of Lewes hold the Blessing of the Fleet?

A. May.

———

Q. What union gathering place in Wilmington's Southbridge neighborhood was also used for dances, shows, and other entertainment?

A. Longshoremen's Hall.

———

Q. When the precursor of the Delaware Symphony Orchestra was founded in the late-nineteenth century by Alfred I. du Pont, where did the musicians practice?

A. A machine shop.

Q. In what year did Wilmington's annual Greek Festival begin?

A. 1966.

Q. What is the name of the weekend entertainment pull-out tabloid published by the *News Journal* every Friday?

A. *55 Hours.*

Q. What private organization recently developed a Wilmington exhibit about Hebrew merchants?

A. Jewish Historical Society of Delaware.

Q. The colorful December celebration in Delaware's Swedish community, including a church procession and a crown of candles, honors what saint?

A. Lucia.

Q. Delaware's only all-news radio station has what call letters?

A. WILM-AM.

Q. In May 1909 the Wilmington Orchestra gave a benefit concert to raise money for what naval endeavor?

A. A silver service for the battleship *Delaware*.

Q. In what year was Wilmington's Polish Library Association founded?

A. 1898.

Q. Where is the Governor's Fall Festival and fair held each year?

A. Woodburn Mansion, Dover.

Q. In which Delaware city do the Second Street Players perform?

A. Milford.

Q. At public dances in Delaware taverns in the early 1700s, what instrument usually supplied the music?

A. Fiddle.

Q. Until a fire in 1934 caused extensive damage, what was situated along Shellpot Creek at Philadelphia Pike near Wilmington?

A. An amusement park.

Q. The Golden Blues, Visions, Deltones, Y Chromes, and Overtones perform what style of music at the University of Delaware?

A. A cappella singing.

Q. The annual food-and-entertainment festival held in early June at Eighth and Broom Streets in Wilmington focuses on what ethnic group?

A. Greeks.

Q. The entertainment center at Brandywine Town Center in northern Delaware had what name?

A. FunScape.

Q. What public house stood on the southeast corner of Third and Market Streets in Wilmington during the American Revolution?

A. Sign of the Ship.

———⊗⊗⊙———

Q. Where in Dover can the public see displays of law-enforcement and crime paraphernalia?

A. Delaware State Police Museum.

———⊗⊗⊙———

Q. Late in his life, much-honored musician Cab Calloway lived in which community?

A. Hockessin.

———⊗⊗⊙———

Q. The Delaware Symphony plays an annual New Year's Eve concert in the Grand Opera House featuring music of what European city ?

A. Vienna.

———⊗⊗⊙———

Q. When did Delaware public schools begin instruction in playing musical instruments?

A. 1928.

———⊗⊗⊙———

Q. For what rock song was Delaware's George Thorogood known in the 1980s?

A. "Bad to the Bone."

Q. The annual Camelot Ball benefits what private agency that operates shelters and conducts programs to help children?

A. Child, Inc.

Q. Which two stars were featured in the movie *Beloved*, partly filmed in New Castle in 1997?

A. Oprah Winfrey and Danny Glover.

Q. Where amid Brandywine Hundred's suburban sprawl can shoppers find a rural oasis selling farm goods and produce?

A. Highland Orchards.

Q. What Catholic Church, the focus of Polish-American life in Wilmington, holds an annual festival?

A. Saint Hedwig's.

Q. Cleveland Morris was co-founder of what professional acting troupe?

A. Delaware Theater Company.

Q. Mark R. Lawlor wrote a history of what suburban Wilmington center of entertainment at the turn of the twentieth century?

A. Brandywine Springs Amusement Park.

Q. The theater that operates in a hall on Miller's Road, Ardentown, has what name?

A. Candlelight Music Dinner Theatre.

———— ∞∞ ————

Q. Which thirteen-year-old boy wrote a musical elegy on the death of President John F. Kennedy and conducted its Wilmington Symphony performance?

A. Stefan Kozinski.

———— ∞∞ ————

Q. In the year 2000, Wilmington's annual Polish Festival was how old?

A. Forty-four years.

———— ∞∞ ————

Q. What rock 'n' roll Hall of Famer was almost killed in an auto accident on U.S. 13 near Dover in 1956?

A. Carl Perkins.

———— ∞∞ ————

Q. Delaware's Beatrice "Bebe" Coker filled what role in the local arts scene?

A. Playwright.

———— ∞∞ ————

Q. What two Wilmington organizations were merged in the 1920s to form the Delaware Symphony Orchestra?

A. Music School and Symphony Club.

Q. Around 1654, what Dutch colonial governor built Delaware's first theater, described as a "pleasure house"?

A. Johan Printz.

———◦◦◦———

Q. For more than a half-century, what Newark group has been performing comedy and drama?

A. Chapel Street Players.

———◦◦◦———

Q. New York artist Arlene Boehm wrote a children's book called *Jack in Search of Art*, featuring what furry creature touring the Delaware Art Museum?

A. A bear.

———◦◦◦———

Q. Reenactors take on historic roles for what annual event at Fort Delaware State Park?

A. Garrison Weekend.

———◦◦◦———

Q. The annual Delaware Coast Day in Lewes features what sort of culinary competition?

A. Crab cookoff.

———◦◦◦———

Q. What southern rock group, whose name roughly rhymes with Tin Lizzard, has performed at Wilmington's Big Kahuna nightclub?

A. Lynyrd Skynyrd.

Q. Seasonal family theatrical entertainment geared for the younger beach set may be seen where?

A. Rehoboth Summer Children's Theatre.

Q. Award winners Georgia and Mark Marquisee of Arden work in what entertainment medium?

A. Filmmaking.

Q. Lewes, a year-round beach community and Delaware's oldest town, offers how many shops and restaurants?

A. Approximately forty.

Q. What traveling circus has provided four decades of entertainment in Delaware?

A. Clyde Beatty–Cole Brothers.

Q. For eight decades, what yuletime event held at the DuPont Country Club has benefited nonprofit groups?

A. The Christmas Shop.

Q. The first Delaware Independent Film Festival, with movies from fifteen countries, was held in 1998 in what city?

A. Rehoboth Beach.

Q. What state agency supports the Mid-Atlantic Chamber Music Society?

A. Delaware Division of the Arts.

—⊗⊗⊗—

Q. What Dover actress played in *Northern Exposure* and the movie *Mystery Date*?

A. Teri Polo.

—⊗⊗⊗—

Q. New Castle's historic nineteenth-century Opera House, originally a meeting hall, was converted for what use around 1885?

A. Roller skating.

—⊗⊗⊗—

Q. Delaware's only vineyard and winery, located near Lewes, has what name?

A. Nassau Valley.

—⊗⊗⊗—

Q. Delaware's Egyptian community holds an annual fete at what Red Lion Church?

A. Saint Mary Coptic Orthodox.

—⊗⊗⊗—

Q. What rock 'n' roll band is made up of law-enforcement officers from Delaware?

A. First State Force.

Q. Dolphin-watching excursions are available from which Delaware seaside town?

A. Lewes.

Q. Where in the Hotel du Pont are the most elegant high-society formal dances and cotillions held?

A. Gold Ballroom.

Q. Historic home tours are among the spring festivities at what event in the capital?

A. Old Dover Days.

Q. What is the name of the popular replica of Delaware's Swedish colonial tall ship, a major tourist attraction?

A. *Kalmar Nyckel.*

HISTORY

C H A P T E R T H R E E

Q. In what year did pioneers from Sweden and Finland found the first permanent European settlement in the Delaware Valley at what is now Wilmington?

A. 1638.

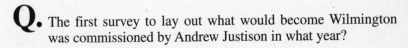

Q. The first survey to lay out what would become Wilmington was commissioned by Andrew Justison in what year?

A. 1730.

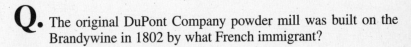

Q. The original DuPont Company powder mill was built on the Brandywine in 1802 by what French immigrant?

A. Eleuthère Irénée du Pont.

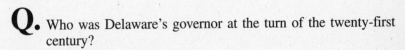

Q. Who was Delaware's governor at the turn of the twenty-first century?

A. Thomas R. Carper.

Q. In what year was the Delaware Air National Guard founded?

A. 1946.

Q. What historic building stands at the foot of French Street on the Christina River in Wilmington?

A. The Amtrak Railroad Station.

Q. What national appointive position did Delaware's Dorothy Elston Kabis hold from 1969 to 1971?

A. U.S. Treasurer.

Q. What two ships from Sweden brought the first settlers to what is now Wilmington?

A. *Kalmar Nyckel* and *Fogel Grip*.

Q. Wilmington College has been holding classes in which historic Wilmington building for more than a decade?

A. Old Custom House.

Q. What structure once stood at the site of the present Acme supermarket adjacent to Trolley Square in Wilmington?

A. Baltimore and Ohio Railroad Station.

Q. Who led the first Delaware Regiment in 1776?

A. Colonel John Haslet.

Q. Where did Naamans Creek and Naamans Road get their names?

A. From an Indian chief.

Q. In what year did the British occupy Wilmington and loot the state treasury?

A. 1777.

Q. In 1663 what group headed by Peter Plockhoy set up a colony at what is now Lewes?

A. Mennonites.

Q. In the early nineteenth century where did the federal courts meet in Delaware?

A. New Castle Town Hall.

Q. The Wilmington thoroughfare now known as Martin Luther King Jr. Boulevard had what earlier name?

A. Front Street.

Q. What ominous warning was printed on the back of Delaware's colonial shilling?

A. "To counterfeit is death."

Q. Who founded the town of Newport in 1735?

A. John Justis.

Q. How tall did a man have to be to join the Wilmington police force under the charter of 1883?

A. Five feet, four inches.

Q. In the 1730s Andrew Justison's son-in-law Thomas Willing gave what name to his tract of land when he started what would become Wilmington?

A. Willingtown.

Q. Where did Delaware get its name?

A. From Lord De La Warr, governor of Virginia in 1610.

Q. What Wilmington native and long-time federal judge ordered desegregation of the University of Delaware in 1952?

A. Collins J. Seitz.

Q. Who was Wilmington's first African-American mayor?

A. Dr. James H. Sills Jr.

Q. In 1673 the Delaware River colony under the Dutch had what three county seats?

A. Chester, New Castle, and Lewes.

Q. During a difficult eighteenth-century voyage to America, what sort of meat was the du Pont family forced to eat?

A. Rat.

Q. The annual celebration marking the date Delaware broke away from English rule has what name?

A. Separation Day.

Q. Before Delaware had a governor, what was the state chief executive's title?

A. President.

———— ❦ ————

Q. In the 1600s, who was Delaware's first medical practitioner?

A. Dr. Tymon Stidham.

———— ❦ ————

Q. Wilmington's Brandywine Zoological Gardens opened in what year?

A. 1904.

———— ❦ ————

Q. The first volunteer fire company in the state, organized in Wilmington in December 1775, chose what name?

A. Friendship.

———— ❦ ————

Q. In what year did Pierre S. "Pete" du Pont make his bid for the U.S. presidential nomination?

A. 1988.

———— ❦ ————

Q. Before 1861, when federal money was first printed, the Bank of Delaware issued what unusual denomination of currency?

A. A three-dollar bill.

———— ❦ ————

Q. Delaware revolutionary hero Caesar Rodney's image was once placed on what U.S. Postal Service product?

A. Nine-cent postcard.

Q. How much did it cost to build Delaware's tall ship *Kalmar Nyckel*?

A. $3.2 million.

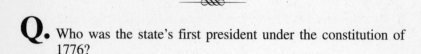

Q. What was the only skirmish on Delaware soil during the Revolutionary War?

A. Battle of Cooch's Bridge (1777).

Q. Who was the state's first president under the constitution of 1776?

A. John McKinly.

Q. In what year did the Fenwick Island Lighthouse begin operations?

A. 1859.

Q. The state constitution of 1776 provided for what two representative houses?

A. Assembly and Legislative Council.

Q. What Wilmington soldier was the state's only fatality in the Persian Gulf War of 1991?

A. Sergeant James McCoy, U.S. Army.

Q. In the 1730s, what motivated Quaker Elizabeth Shipley to move her family to what is now Wilmington?

A. A dream.

Q. Delaware first came under British rule in what year?

A. 1664.

Q. On what date in 1776 did Delaware vote to separate from English domination?

A. June 15.

Q. What is Delaware's only Hebrew high school, situated at the Jewish Community Center in Talleyville?

A. Gratz.

Q. How many officers did the original state Highway Traffic Police have in 1919 to patrol Philadelphia Pike?

A. One.

Q. African-Americans in Delaware celebrate what early summer event to mark the end of slavery in 1865?

A. Juneteenth.

Q. What three men signed the Declaration of Independence for Delaware?

A. Caesar Rodney, George Read, and Thomas McKean.

Q. What was the annual salary of a Wilmington police constable in 1883?

A. $720.

Q. George Washington and other Revolutionary War notables are said to have stayed in what Claymont-area structure, built around 1723?

A. Robinson House.

Q. What lawyer and patriot served as Delaware's president in 1781 and 1782 and was a member of the Constitutional Convention in 1787?

A. John Dickinson.

Q. Bethany Beach, established in 1901, was originally used for what kind of gatherings?

A. Church retreats.

Q. In what year was the private Brandywine Academy founded in Brandywine Village?

A. 1798.

Q. On what dates did Caesar Rodney make his famous ride to Philadelphia to declare Delaware independent from England?

A. July 1–2, 1776.

Q. William J. Winchester, the first African-American elected to the state House of Representatives in 1948 is memorialized by what Wilmington structure?

A. Third Street Bridge.

Q. What Chinese-born physics professor was a lieutenant governor of Delaware in the 1980s?

A. S. B. Woo.

Q. In 1977 who was hired as Wilmington's first woman police officer?

A. Golden Wilson.

Q. During the presidential election of 1860, in which Republican Abraham Lincoln ran on an anti-slavery platform, what candidate received Delaware's electoral votes?

A. John C. Breckinridge, a Southern Democrat.

Q. Besides serving as a roadway, the Van Buren Street Bridge, which opened in Wilmington in 1907, functioned as what type of conduit?

A. Aqueduct.

Q. Delaware became the three southern counties of what territory in 1682?

A. Pennsylvania.

Q. Revolutionary patriot and lawyer George Read of Delaware was admitted to the bar at what age?

A. Nineteen.

Q. What was the name of the ship that brought the du Ponts to the United States near the start of the nineteenth century?

A. *American Eagle.*

———⊗∞∞⊗———

Q. What was the nickname of New Castle's whipping post?

A. Red Hannah.

———⊗∞∞⊗———

Q. The first six women were admitted to Delaware College, now the University of Delaware, in what year?

A. 1872.

———⊗∞∞⊗———

Q. What Delaware-born "Hero of Lake Champlain" defeated the British at the battle of Plattsburgh in 1814?

A. Commodore Thomas Macdonough.

———⊗∞∞⊗———

Q. During the Civil War, Fort Delaware functioned primarily as what type of facility?

A. A prison for Confederate soldiers.

———⊗∞∞⊗———

Q. Delaware's constitution of 1776 specifically outlawed what inhumane colonial practice?

A. The importation of slaves.

———⊗∞∞⊗———

Q. When was Cape Henlopen Lighthouse originally built?

A. 1764.

Q. Wilmington eventually took its name from what English lord?

A. Spencer Compton, earl of Wilmington.

———∞∞∞———

Q. Caesar Rodney held what office when he made his famous "independence" ride to Philadelphia in 1776?

A. Speaker of the Delaware Assembly.

———∞∞∞———

Q. How many prisoners were held at Fort Delaware during the Civil War?

A. Forty thousand.

———∞∞∞———

Q. Sergeant James P. Connor of Delaware was decorated with which military award for heroism in World War II?

A. The Congressional Medal of Honor.

———∞∞∞———

Q. In what year did Swedish Delaware fall to the Dutch under Peter Stuyvesant?

A. 1655.

———∞∞∞———

Q. Approximately how many men from Delaware were sent to Europe to fight in World War I?

A. Seventy-five hundred.

———∞∞∞———

Q. Founded in 1867, what was Delaware's first secondary school for African Americans?

A. Howard High, in Wilmington.

Q. What Revolutionary War–era figure became Delaware's first judicial chancellor?

A. William Killen.

———⊗⊗⊗———

Q. Under the state constitution of 1792, which eliminated the presidential system, who became Delaware's first governor?

A. Joshua Clayton.

———⊗⊗⊗———

Q. In what year was the last man punished at the Delaware whipping post?

A. 1952.

———⊗⊗⊗———

Q. Gregory M. Sleet was sworn in as Delaware's first African-American U.S. district court judge in what year?

A. 1998.

———⊗⊗⊗———

Q. In what year was the Delaware State Police Canine Unit founded?

A. 1925.

———⊗⊗⊗———

Q. To avoid antitrust action, in 1912, the DuPont Company spun off which two new powder companies?

A. Hercules and Atlas.

———⊗⊗⊗———

Q. British cannons bombarded Lewes in what year?

A. 1813.

Q. What former DuPont Company and General Motors officer, a Claymont resident, built the Empire State Building in New York City?

A. John Jacob Raskob.

———&———

Q. By 1905 approximately how many motor vehicles were registered in Delaware?

A. Three hundred.

———&———

Q. What object was used in the 1920s at selected Delaware gas stations to indicate the need for a state trooper by a local citizen?

A. A red flag.

———&———

Q. What ship brought William Penn to Delaware in 1682?

A. *Welcome.*

———&———

Q. How many men were on the Wilmington police force in 1880?

A. Fifty.

———&———

Q. In what year did England's colonial governor grant Wilmington a borough charter?

A. 1739.

———&———

Q. When is Delaware Day celebrated?

A. December 7.

Q. Where did Delaware delegates meet in 1787 to ratify the U.S. Constitution?

A. Battell's Tavern, Dover.

Q. In what year were women given the right to vote in Delaware?

A. 1920.

Q. Which building was the colonial capitol for Delaware from 1732 to 1777?

A. New Castle Court House.

Q. What historic Coast Guard ship was tied in the Christina River at King Street in the 1980s?

A. *Mohawk.*

Q. Delaware became the first state by ratifying the U.S. Constitution on what date?

A. December 7, 1787.

Q. What was the early vocation of Thomas Fenwick, who gave his name to Fenwick Island?

A. Pirate.

Q. When was Dover's Christ Episcopal Church built?

A. 1734.

Q. In what year was present-day Lewes settled by the Dutch as a whaling colony?

A. 1631.

———⊗———

Q. When was Mount Lebanon United Methodist Church near Talleyville built?

A. 1834.

———⊗———

Q. What was an early name for Frederica, founded in 1770?

A. Johnny Cake Landing.

———⊗———

Q. A Capuchin brother, Ronald Giannone, founded what Wilmington charitable organization in 1977 to feed the poor?

A. Ministry of Caring.

———⊗———

Q. Who led the Sussex County Loyalists, who didn't want independence from England?

A. Thomas Robinson.

———⊗———

Q. Wilmington's white-uniformed street cleaners, who manned large-wheeled buckets around the turn of the twentieth century, had what nickname?

A. White Wings.

———⊗———

Q. In what year was the Wilmington Marine Terminal built?

A. 1923.

Q. About half the settlers of New Sweden on the Christina in 1638 were from what European country other than Sweden?

A. Finland.

———✺———

Q. What is the modern name of the former Quaker community known in the early 1700s as Duck Creek Village?

A. Smyrna.

———✺———

Q. What Sussex County woman belonged to a gang that kidnapped free Delaware blacks and sold them into slavery in the South?

A. Patty Cannon.

———✺———

Q. How much did the Wilmington Board of Education spend per child during the year 1900?

A. $20.48.

———✺———

Q. Approximately how many Delawareans fought with the Union army during the Civil War?

A. Thirteen thousand.

———✺———

Q. Where was the first seventeenth-century Swedish church built in the Wilmington area?

A. Crane Hook on the Delaware.

Q. Dobbinsville, a late nineteenth-century New Castle area ironworkers's neighborhood, got its name from what builder?

A. Richard J. Dobbins.

Q. What unusual form of revenue developed in low-lying areas of the state from the need to drain marshland and maintain runoff channels?

A. Ditch taxes.

Q. Who was the first pastor of Wilmington's seventeenth-century Old Swedes Church?

A. Ericus Bjork.

Q. E. I. du Pont served as president of the DuPont Company during what years?

A. 1802–1834.

Q. What was the name of Wilmington's first big hotel, built at Fifth and Market Streets in 1873 with more than one hundred rooms?

A. Clayton House.

Q. How many Delaware men joined the Confederate army during the Civil War?

A. Approximately five hundred.

Q. Wilmington's nineteenth-century Fire Station No. 5 on Gilpin Avenue was originally used by what volunteer company?

A. Water Witch.

———∞———

Q. What was the former name of Wilmington's now-demolished Memorial Hospital?

A. Homeopathic.

———∞———

Q. Who was Delaware's first African-American attorney?

A. Louis L. Redding.

———∞———

Q. Senator John J. Williams was from what Delaware town?

A. Millsboro.

———∞———

Q. During the early 1800s, what Irish-born Roman Catholic priest almost single-handedly formed the Catholic community in northern Delaware?

A. Father Patrick Kenny.

———∞———

Q. In October 1890, what calamitous event claimed twelve lives and razed thirty Wilmington homes?

A. The DuPont Company powder explosion.

———∞———

Q. In the early twentieth century, officials of the town of Bethel had its streets paved with what material?

A. Oyster shells.

Q. What two houses comprise the Delaware General Assembly?

A. Senate and House of Representatives.

Q. What civil rights pioneer and former state NAACP president taught the "Tuskegee Airmen" to fly during World War II?

A. Littleton P. Mitchell.

Q. In what year did Wilmington police first establish a detective bureau?

A. 1914.

Q. In the mid-1800s, Wilmington night watchmen looked for fires from what vantage point?

A. Cupola of Old Town Hall.

Q. What Delawarean was the last Union general to be killed in the Civil War?

A. Thomas Smyth.

Q. Irish-born John McKinly, who became Delaware's first president, had what profession?

A. Physician.

Q. What was Henry Hudson looking for when he discovered Delaware Bay in 1609?

A. A passage to the Far East.

Q. How many members sit in the state senate?

A. Twenty-one.

———

Q. What U.S. senator from Delaware has his name attached to an important government-backed savings plan?

A. William V. Roth Jr. (Roth IRA).

———

Q. The land near Naamans Creek on the Delaware-Pennsylvania line was a popular site for what illegal activity in the early 1800s?

A. Dueling.

———

Q. Before the advent of electricity, what group of city workers took care of street lighting in Wilmington?

A. Gas lamplighters.

———

Q. What notorious New York thieves were caught in Wilmington in 1873 trying to rob the Bank of Delaware?

A. Big Frank McCoy Gang.

———

Q. Members of what religious group spirited runaway slaves through Delaware to freedom in the North?

A. Quakers.

———

Q. Which historic Wilmington court continued to handle capital cases until the early twentieth century?

A. Oyer and Terminer.

Q. For whom is the town of Dagsboro named?

A. General John Dagworthy.

Q. How many members sit in the state house of representatives?

A. Forty-one.

Q. Founded in 1748 and still in operation, what is the oldest school in Delaware?

A. Wilmington Friends School.

Q. In what year did Delaware pass its General Incorporation Law, making it easy to incorporate without the special legislative charters required elsewhere?

A. 1899.

Q. President Franklin D. Roosevelt visited Wilmington in 1938 for what reason?

A. The three hundredth anniversary of the Swedish landing.

Q. What was the name of the first institution of learning in Newark, opened in 1767?

A. Newark Academy.

Q. What African American was elected to the state senate in 1964?

A. Herman M. Holloway Sr.

Q. In what year did the three counties of Delaware begin governing themselves?

A. 1704.

———⟨∞⟩———

Q. Delaware State Hospital south of Wilmington is often known by what name taken from a nearby nineteenth-century railway station?

A. Farnhurst.

———⟨∞⟩———

Q. Who was the first official mayor of the new city of Wilmington in 1832?

A. Richard H. Bayard.

———⟨∞⟩———

Q. Which member of a prominent Delaware family was awarded the Congressional Medal of Honor for heroism in the Civil War?

A. Henry Algernon du Pont.

———⟨∞⟩———

Q. A Delaware governor may be impeached for committing high crimes or misdemeanors, treason, or what other offense?

A. Bribery.

———⟨∞⟩———

Q. While New Castle and Sussex Counties are governed by councils, what governing system does Kent County retain?

A. Levy court.

Q. How many chief executives did Delaware have before Gov. Thomas R. Carper?

A. Seventy.

Q. What towering structure now stands on the site of the Green Tree Inn, an 1850s tavern of ill repute in the Brandywine Village area of Wilmington?

A. Cathedral Church of Saint John.

Q. How many lashes were given to a burglar when the whipping post was last used in 1952?

A. Twenty.

Q. In 1793 what epidemic drove people into Delaware from the North?

A. Yellow fever.

Q. In what year did the early du Ponts sail from France to England to begin new lives?

A. 1799.

Q. What son of a U.S. president married Ethel du Pont in Wilmington in June 1937?

A. Franklin D. Roosevelt Jr.

Q. Legend says Pea Patch Island got its name when it was formed by what?

A. A shipwrecked cargo of peas.

———— ∞ ————

Q. Who was the first African American chosen for jury duty in Delaware, in 1900?

A. Moses America.

———— ∞ ————

Q. Wilmington began using paid fire fighters in what year?

A. 1921.

———— ∞ ————

Q. Wilmington's Harlan and Hollingsworth Company made what new kind of vessel for the Union navy during the Civil War?

A. Ironclad.

———— ∞ ————

Q. What controversial British sympathizer of the Revolutionary War was hanged in Dover in 1788 amid public protest?

A. Cheyney Clow.

———— ∞ ————

Q. In what year did the former Dutch settlement of New Amstel officially become New Castle under the English?

A. 1664.

———— ∞ ————

Q. "The Conscience of the Senate" was a term applied to which U.S. senator from Delaware who served from 1946 to 1970?

A. John J. Williams.

Q. How many representatives does Delaware have in Congress?

A. One.

———⚬⚬⚬———

Q. When did construction begin on Old Swede's Church in Wilmington?

A. 1698.

———⚬⚬⚬———

Q. What was the occupation of James Adams, the first of his profession to work in Delaware, beginning in 1761?

A. Printer.

———⚬⚬⚬———

Q. In what year did marine archaeologists raise the sunken eighteenth-century ship HMS *DeBraak*?

A. 1986.

———⚬⚬⚬———

Q. When was Ezion Methodist Episcopal Church, the first church for African-Americans in Delaware, founded in Wilmington?

A. 1805.

———⚬⚬⚬———

Q. Voters in Delaware who do not choose a political party and register as nonpartisans are known by what name?

A. Declines.

———⚬⚬⚬———

Q. Who was the first chief justice of Delaware, serving from 1764 to 1770?

A. John Vining.

Q. What Irish immigrant to Wilmington worked as a ship's carpenter before earning the Congressional Medal of Honor in the Civil War?

A. Bernard McCarren.

———⌘———

Q. How many Delawareans served in the armed forces during World War II?

A. Around thirty thousand.

———⌘———

Q. General John Dagworthy was granted a twenty-thousand-acre tract of land in 1759 at the head of Pepper Creek for his service in what war?

A. French and Indian.

———⌘———

Q. What distinction did Wilmington native Edward T. Demby achieve in 1918 with the Protestant Episcopal Church in Arkansas?

A. First African-American Suffragan Bishop.

———⌘———

Q. After World War II, what local aviator founded Summit Aviation, a successful airport and aircraft services business near Middletown?

A. Richard C. "Kip" DuPont Jr.

———⌘———

Q. Born in 1796, John M. Clayton, a judge, U.S. senator, and U.S. secretary of state who lived in Buena Vista mansion on U.S. 13, was famous for cooking what special meat dish?

A. Turtle.

Q. The portly seventeenth-century governor of New Sweden on the Delaware, Johan Printz, is believed to have weighed how many pounds?

A. Four hundred.

Q. Dravo Corporation built how many ships on the Christina River during World War II?

A. Two hundred.

Q. How many Congressional Medals of Honor have been awarded to Delawareans?

A. Fourteen.

Q. What is the meaning of the Delaware Indian name *Lenni Lenape*?

A. "Original people."

Q. Where did members of the Delaware National Guard's artillery unit serve together during World War II?

A. Bora Bora.

Q. A Wilmington street was named for what businessman and delegate to the Constitutional Convention in 1787?

A. Jacob Broom.

Q. The Reverend Peter Spencer of Wilmington (1782–1843) founded what new religious denomination in 1813?

A. Union Church of Africans.

———∞———

Q. What Delaware governor supported woman suffrage in 1916, four years before the Twenty-first Amendment mandated it?

A. John G. Townsend Jr.

———∞———

Q. Who was captain of the *Kalmar Nyckel* when it arrived on its first journey to Delaware in 1638?

A. Peter Minuit.

———∞———

Q. The Bank of Delaware, now PNC Bank, was founded in what year?

A. 1795.

———∞———

Q. In what year did the Great Fire destroy many waterfront buildings in New Castle?

A. 1824.

———∞———

Q. In the 1980s what statute removed restrictions on credit card interest rates, spurring a banking boom in Delaware?

A. Financial Center Development Act.

Q. Who served as an interim governor for seventeen days in 1993?

A. Dale E. Wolf.

Q. In the late 1600s, what menace plagued Delaware coastal communities?

A. Pirates.

Q. In what year did the Delaware National Guard patrol Wilmington following riots?

A. 1968.

Q. Mount Cuba near Wilmington derived its name from what eighteenth-century estate of Irish immigrant Cornelius Hallahan?

A. Cuba Rock.

Q. Cannonballs from the British bombardment of Lewes in the War of 1812 are said to have claimed what lone casualty?

A. A chicken.

Q. A statue of two soldiers, erected in 1998 in Brandywine Park, Wilmington, honors what national group of heroes?

A. The eighty-six African-American Medal of Honor winners.

Q. On what present-day site did Continental troops encamp in 1777 to protect Wilmington from the British?

A. Lovering Avenue near Broom Street.

Q. Delaware's Emily P. Bissel, born in 1861, originated what national holiday tradition to benefit tuberculosis patients?

A. Christmas seals.

Q. Swedish merchants sent their sailing vessels to what is now Delaware in the 1600s to fetch which two much-in-demand commodities?

A. Furs and tobacco.

Q. Where was the first bell for Wilmington's Old Swedes Church placed?

A. Oak Tree.

Q. In the 1790s who built the stately Georgian mansion Woodburn, now the governor's residence in Dover?

A. Charles Hillyard III.

Q. What was the original purpose of Jacob Broom's ninety-five-acre estate on the Brandywine that was sold to the du Ponts for making gunpowder?

A. Cotton Mill.

Q. During the American Revolution, most of Delaware's British sympathizers lived in what area?

A. Sussex County.

Q. Among the U.S. delegation to formulate the Treaty of Ghent ending the War of 1812 was what senator from Wilmington?

A. James A. Bayard.

Q. Benjamin Franklin was one of the consultants in 1786 on what major public works project that was built the next century in Delaware?

A. Chesapeake and Delaware Canal.

Q. During the Civil War, where did most of the Delawareans who sided with the Confederacy live?

A. Sussex County.

Q. What sort of factory did Joseph Bancroft build along the Brandywine in 1831?

A. Cotton mill.

Q. In which Revolutionary War engagement of September 1777 was the American flag first carried before troops?

A. The Battle of Cooches Bridge.

Q. In slaveholding times Woodburn, now the governor's home, was used as part of what escape route?

A. Underground Railroad.

―――∞∞∞―――

Q. Where in Dover was a portrait of the British King George III publicly burned in 1776?

A. The Green.

―――∞∞∞―――

Q. America's first murder-by-mail case, which claimed the lives of two Doverites in 1898, involved what foodstuff?

A. Poisoned chocolates.

―――∞∞∞―――

Q. Delaware City, a trim town on the Delaware River, was known by what name when it was founded in 1801?

A. Newbold's Landing.

―――∞∞∞―――

Q. Senator Joseph R. Biden Jr., launched a brief presidential campaign in what election year?

A. 1988.

―――∞∞∞―――

Q. What is the name of the first woman ever to be elected governor of Delaware, in 2000?

A. Ruth Ann Minner.

ARTS & LITERATURE

C H A P T E R F O U R

Q. What is the term for the turn-of-the-twentieth-century art tradition characterized by painters from the Wilmington area?

A. Brandywine School.

———⊗∞⊗———

Q. Who wrote the massive 1888 *History of Delaware*?

A. J. Thomas Scharf.

———⊗∞⊗———

Q. What beloved, bearded twentieth-century Wilmington journalist spent more than fifty years writing for the city's newspapers?

A. William P. Frank.

———⊗∞⊗———

Q. In what year did the Delaware College of Art and Design open its doors on Wilmington's Market Street Mall?

A. 1997.

———⊗∞⊗———

Q. The statewide *Sunday News Journal* reached what landmark circulation figure in 1992?

A. 150,000.

Q. Delaware artist Frank Schoonover studied under what legendary local painter?

A. Howard Pyle.

———⊗———

Q. The Delaware Art Museum began as what Wilmington "society"?

A. Fine Arts.

———⊗———

Q. The *Wilmington News Journal* traces its history through what three earlier newspapers?

A. *Morning News*, *Journal-Every Evening*, and *Evening Journal*.

———⊗———

Q. Reminiscences of Rehoboth Beach are shared by author Virginia Tanzer in what book?

A. *Seagulls Hate Parsnips*.

———⊗———

Q. The *Transcript* newspaper is published in what Delaware municipality?

A. Middletown.

———⊗———

Q. Who wrote his reminiscences in the 1977 book *The Horse on Rodney Square*?

A. Charles Lee Reese Jr.

———⊗———

Q. In 1860 the former John Dickinson property at Eighth and Market Streets in Wilmington became the site of what structure?

A. Wilmington Institute Library.

Q. What educational institution did Victorine du Pont Bauduy begin in 1817 near Wilmington?

A. Brandywine Manufacturers' Sunday School.

———∞∞∞———

Q. What was Dover's first newspaper, begun in 1802?

A. *Federal Ark.*

———∞∞∞———

Q. Who authored the little volume of historical stories called *Lantern on Lewes*?

A. Hazel D. Brittingham.

———∞∞∞———

Q. Who wrote the 1937 book *Wilmington, Delaware: Three Centuries Under Four Flags*?

A. Anna T. Lincoln.

———∞∞∞———

Q. What nineteenth-century Claymont artist illustrated works by Charles Dickens and William Shakespeare?

A. Felix O. C. Darley.

———∞∞∞———

Q. What widely circulated local magazine includes general feature articles and covers the state's social scene?

A. *Delaware Today.*

———∞∞∞———

Q. What Newark newspaper was founded by Everett C. Johnson in 1910?

A. The *Post.*

Q. Girls in Delaware had an opportunity to receive a college education at their own school when what institution opened in Newark in 1914?

A. Women's College.

———— ✸ ————

Q. What Wilmington female artist, with connections in the U.S. capital, has for thirty years been known for her oil paintings on garden themes?

A. Mary Page Evans.

———— ✸ ————

Q. Delaware-based corporations including Wilmington Trust Company and MBNA have widely invested in what locally produced commodity?

A. Paintings.

———— ✸ ————

Q. What tabloid newspaper for lawyers was first published in 1998?

A. *Delaware Law Weekly.*

———— ✸ ————

Q. A statue of what army aviator who commanded the Women's Auxiliary Ferrying Squadron in World War II stands at New Castle County Airport?

A. Nancy Love.

———— ✸ ————

Q. What Revolutionary War patriot wrote his ideas about independence in *Letters from a Farmer*?

A. John Dickinson.

Q. Virginia M. Burdick wrote a 1991 book about what Delaware navel hero?

A. Capt. Thomas Macdonough.

Q. What Delaware illustrator provided free art lessons for talented students?

A. Howard Pyle.

Q. The site of the Wilmington Institute Free Library at Tenth and Market Streets was once used for what purpose?

A. Old First Presbyterian Church cemetery.

Q. Who is depicted on the back of the Delaware quarter?

A. Caesar Rodney on horseback.

Q. Cy Liberman and James Rosbrow wrote what 1954 book, much reprinted, explaining how state government works?

A. *The Delaware Citizen.*

Q. The Delaware College of Art and Design in Wilmington is a partnership between which two U.S. art schools?

A. Corcoran and Pratt Institute.

Q. Wilmington's first Jewish community was described in the 1999 book *Becoming American, Remaining Jewish* by what author?

A. Toni Young.

———— ∞∞∞ ————

Q. What is the largest commercial bookselling establishment in center-city Wilmington?

A. Ninth Street Book Shop.

———— ∞∞∞ ————

Q. What female Delaware painter in the 1920s helped to found the Delaware Academy of Art?

A. Henryette Stadelman Whiteside.

———— ∞∞∞ ————

Q. What landscape artist was born in Brandywine Village in 1829 of a prominent family?

A. Henry Lea Tatnall.

———— ∞∞∞ ————

Q. Where in Wilmington is the Howard Pyle art studio?

A. 1305 North Franklin Street.

———— ∞∞∞ ————

Q. Delawarean Eric Zencey wrote what 1995 best-selling first novel?

A. *Panama.*

Q. What nineteenth-century Delaware artist etched a well-known picture of the covered bridge that once crossed the Brandywine at Market Street?

A. Robert Shaw.

———— ∞∞ ————

Q. What popular weekly newspaper at the Delaware seashore was named after a large sea creature?

A. The *Whale*.

———— ∞∞ ————

Q. Local artist Frank Jefferis painted what oil-on-canvas seaside scene displayed in the Delaware Supreme Court office?

A. *Cape Henlopen Light House*.

———— ∞∞ ————

Q. Nine northern Delaware women artists who support each other and exhibit together are collectively known by what name?

A. The X-Girls.

———— ∞∞ ————

Q. What modern Delaware artist was best known for his pictures of life in the West?

A. Gayle P. Hoskins.

———— ∞∞ ————

Q. Where in Delaware is the world's largest collection of early American decorative arts?

A. Winterthur Museum.

Q. In what year did the *Wilmington Evening Journal* begin publication?

A. 1886.

Q. What is the name of the 1938 Federal Writers' Project book that describes coastal areas of eastern states, including Delaware?

A. The Ocean Highway.

Q. The annual Delaware Art Museum fundraising soiree has what name?

A. Beaux Arts Ball.

Q. The Wilmington Society of the Fine Arts was formed in 1912 to raise money to buy forty-eight works by what local illustrator?

A. Howard Pyle.

Q. What Dover museum houses the art collection of a Middletown man?

A. Sewell C. Biggs Museum of American Art.

Q. The Louis XVI-style mansion and three-hundred-acre Nemours estate near Wilmington, built by Alfred I. du Pont, resembles a small version of what estate near Paris, France?

A. Versailles.

Q. What book about nineteenth-century slave trading was written by Georgetown-born George Alfred Townsend?

A. *The Entailed Hat.*

Q. What was the name of the Wilmington-based Sunday newspaper of the late nineteenth and early twentieth centuries?

A. *Star.*

Q. A book of reminiscences entitled *This Was Wilmington* was written by what journalist-author?

A. A. O. H. Grier.

Q. The monument at the Rocks on the Christina River commemorating the Swedish Landing of 1638 and dedicated in 1938 was sculpted by whom?

A. Carl Milles.

Q. The decorative front of Wilmington's Grand Opera House is made of what material?

A. Cast iron.

Q. The gardens of the George Read II House on New Castle's Strand were designed about 1840 by whom?

A. Robert Buist.

Q. A picture of the Delaware militia near Noxontown Pond, commanded by Caesar Rodney in 1777, was painted by what twentieth-century artist?

A. Stanley Arthurs.

Q. What types of paintings, including two dozen owned by the state, gained fame for Clawson S. Hammitt?

A. Portraits.

Q. *Wind: How the Flow of Air Has Shaped Life, Myth, and the Land* was written by what former Delaware newspaper reporter?

A. Jan DeBlieu.

Q. Dover's daily *Delaware State News* was first published in what year?

A. 1901.

Q. Where can visitors see displays of doll houses and other children's artifacts dating as far back as 600 B.C.?

A. Delaware Toy and Miniature Museum.

Q. Early in the twentieth century what Delaware judge wrote a three-volume *History of the State of Delaware*?

A. Henry C. Conrad.

Q. What African-American artist from Delaware won recognition in the 1930s for his painting *After a Shower*?

A. Edward Loper Sr.

———⊗⊗⊗———

Q. Where can vacationing beachgoers take art lessons, attend concerts, and view fine arts?

A. Rehoboth Art League.

———⊗⊗⊗———

Q. Who was the Swedish painter, brother of an early rector of Old Swedes Church in Wilmington, who arrived in 1711 and became well known as a portraitist?

A. Gustavus Hesselius.

———⊗⊗⊗———

Q. What Oxford-educated newspaper columnist wrote eloquently and elegantly about people and issues in post–World War II Delaware?

A. Tom Malone.

———⊗⊗⊗———

Q. In the 1920s F. Scott Fitzgerald and his wife, Zelda, lived in what north Wilmington mansion?

A. Ellerslie.

———⊗⊗⊗———

Q. The Delaware Art Museum houses how many works of art?

A. Approximately ten thousand.

Q. What is the name of the Milford newspaper that was started in 1878?

A. *Chronicle.*

———⟨⟩———

Q. Stately Memorial Hall at the University of Delaware, built in 1924, was originally used as what campus facility?

A. Library.

———⟨⟩———

Q. What is the title of the 1911 oil-on-canvas by Frank Schoonover that depicts a man in marshland in a small boat?

A. *Lafitte the Pirate.*

———⟨⟩———

Q. Hendrickson House Museum near Wilmington's Fort Christina dates to what year?

A. 1690.

———⟨⟩———

Q. In 1945 what renowned Delaware artist and his grandson were killed when a train struck their car?

A. N. C. Wyeth.

———⟨⟩———

Q. In the late 1840s what famous American poet lectured at Newark Academy shortly before his death?

A. Edgar Allan Poe.

Q. The bronze sculpture at the U.S. Naval Academy, known to midshipmen as *Tecumseh*, is actually an image of what Delaware Lenni Lenape chieftain of the 1600s?

A. Tamanend.

———⟨⟩———

Q. In 1794 colonial artist and Delaware gentleman farmer Adolph Wertmuller painted a portrait of which American patriot?

A. George Washington.

———⟨⟩———

Q. Who wrote a book in 1898 about old Delaware clockmakers?

A. Henry C. Conrad.

———⟨⟩———

Q. When was the historic Homestead Mansion at the Rehoboth Art League in Henlopen Acres built?

A. Circa 1743.

———⟨⟩———

Q. In 1910 what Delaware artist painted *The Mermaid*, a fanciful, romantic oil-on-canvas?

A. Howard Pyle.

———⟨⟩———

Q. *World War I Remembered*, dealing with Delawareans in the Great War, was written by what local military historian?

A. Major General Francis A. Ianni.

Q. What useful works of art were made by eighteenth-century Delaware craftsmen Duncan Beard and George Crow?

A. Grandfather clocks.

———∞———

Q. While living in Delaware, Zelda Fitzgerald became obsessed with what genre of performing arts?

A. Ballet.

———∞———

Q. In 1803 E. I. du Pont built what elegant Georgian-style home above the banks of the Brandywine?

A. Eleutherian Mills.

———∞———

Q. What unique book gained fame for Delaware's African-American author, editor, poet, and teacher Alice Dunbar Nelson?

A. Her diary.

———∞———

Q. Which two Delaware artists painted scenes from World War I for the *Ladies' Home Journal*?

A. Gayle P. Hoskins and Frank Schoonover.

———∞———

Q. Gertrude F. Dunlap wrote what "folksy" 1990 book about the community north of Wilmington near Edgemoor?

A. *Fox Point Remembered.*

Q. Where can visitors see one of Delaware's first fireproof buildings, built in 1858 of brick and cast iron, to hold state records?

A. Biggs Museum, Dover.

Q. What five-and-dime business formerly occupied the renovated art-deco building that now houses the Delaware History Museum?

A. Woolworth's.

Q. How many Brandywine School paintings, sculptures, and other items are in the University of Delaware's collection?

A. Approximately one thousand.

Q. Older readers can recall "Our Yesterdays" in Emma Mariane's book by that name about rural life in the early 1900s in what community?

A. Brandywine Hundred.

Q. Who wrote *The Swedish Settlements on the Delaware*?

A. Amandus Johnson.

Q. More than a dozen original N. C. Wyeth illustrations are on the third floor of what publicly accessible Wilmington building?

A. The library.

Q. In the 1930s the local antiquarian Joseph Wigglesworth published a book on what subject?

A. Archeological findings of the Lenni-Lenape.

Q. At a Christie's auction in London, the Delaware Art Museum acquired what objects decorated by Dante Gabriel Rossetti and William Morris?

A. Chairs.

Q. What is the name of the library at Wilmington's Latin American Community Center?

A. La Biblioteca del Pueblo.

Q. Carol E. Hoffecker wrote what 1974 book about the historic area along Market Street just north of Eighteenth Street?

A. *Brandywine Village*.

Q. What contemporary Delaware artist created a series of mixed-media collages with titles taken from the works of T. S. Eliot?

A. Rowene MacLeod.

Q. In 1913 who was the first dean of the Women's College of Delaware?

A. Winifred J. Robinson.

Q. A collection of more than two thousand items relating to President Abraham Lincoln's life are housed at which University of Delaware facility in Wilmington?

A. Goodstay Center.

———————

Q. Who wrote the books *Delaware's Medal of Honor Winners* and *Tales of Delaware*?

A. Roger A. Martin.

———————

Q. Which British mystery writer mentions "the American patriot John Dickinson" of Delaware in her novel *A Certain Justice*?

A. P. D. James.

———————

Q. The portrait of Lady Lilith, on permanent display at the Delaware Art Museum, was painted by what nineteenth-century painter and poet?

A. Dante Gabriel Rosetti.

———————

Q. What two ethnic groups are central to C. A. Weslager's 1943 book, *Delaware's Forgotten Folk*?

A. Nanticokes and Moors.

———————

Q. Who was F. Scott Fitzgerald's lifelong Delaware friend from their Princeton University days?

A. U.S. district judge John Biggs.

Q. What is the Delaware state motto?

A. Liberty and Independence.

Q. Journalist William P. "Bill" Frank wrote *God's Impatient Builder*, the story of what beloved Christian minister, in 1972?

A. Reverend James R. Hughes.

Q. Who edited the *History of Delaware, Past and Present*, published in 1929?

A. Wilson Lloyd Bevan.

Q. What 1938 Pulitzer Prize–winning author was born in Wilmington?

A. John P. Marquand.

Q. Which of his novels did F. Scott Fitzgerald work on while living in Delaware?

A. *Tender Is the Night.*

Q. Who wrote the 1969 book *The Log Cabin in America* and a series of books about Delaware Native Americans?

A. Professor C. A. Weslager.

Q. Who is the Wilmington attorney and equestrian who turned a lifelong love of fox hunting into a book entitled *Risk in the Afternoon*?

A. William Prickett.

———◊◊◊———

Q. Who is the retired Temple University music professor who wrote a book about Smyrna, where he grew up?

A. B. Stimson Carrow.

———◊◊◊———

Q. The Wilmington Public Building, the former Post Office, and the Institute Free Library on Rodney Square are built in what architectural style?

A. Greek revival.

———◊◊◊———

Q. A Sussex County native and journalist of the late 1800s, George Alfred Townsend used what pseudonym in his columns?

A. Gath.

———◊◊◊———

Q. N. C. Wyeth's sixty-foot-long mural inside Wilmington's main WSFS bank branch has what title?

A. *The Apotheosis of Family*.

———◊◊◊———

Q. The Wilmington Institute Free Library's interior is decorated with copies of what ancient Greek artwork?

A. Sculpture from the Parthenon (called Elgin Marbles when removed to Great Britain by Lord Elgin).

Q. Frank Zebley's 1947 book contains photos of nearly all of what kind of edifice in Delaware?

A. Churches.

———∞———

Q. Who created the sculpture for Wilmington's Vietnam War Memorial on the Brandywine?

A. Charles Parks.

———∞———

Q. The booklet *Reminiscences of a Town That Thought It Would Be a Metropolis* by William O. Wingate was about what community?

A. Delaware City.

———∞———

Q. The book *Delaware: A Guide to the First State* was published in 1938 as part of what Works Progress Administration endeavor?

A. Federal Writers' Project.

———∞———

Q. What are the given names of the father, son, and grandson in the Wyeth family of artists?

A. N. C., Andrew, and Jamie, respectively.

———∞———

Q. Marjorie G. McNinch wrote what 1966 book that traces the ethnic roots of entertaining in Delaware?

A. *Festivals.*

Q. Around 1750 what Swedish pastor wrote a history of and descriptions about the flourishing settlement in Wilmington?

A. Israel Acrelius.

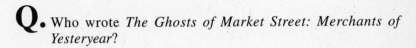

Q. Who wrote *The Ghosts of Market Street: Merchants of Yesteryear?*

A. Ellen Rendle.

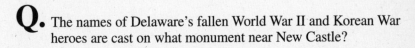

Q. The names of Delaware's fallen World War II and Korean War heroes are cast on what monument near New Castle?

A. Delaware Memorial Bridge Plaza.

Q. In what year did Howard Pyle open his legendary art school in Wilmington?

A. 1900.

Q. The book *Delaware Aviation History* was written by what Dover businessman and Korean War veteran?

A. George J. Frebert.

Q. What Delaware African-American artist, who, like his father, studied at the Barnes Foundation, has exhibited at the Delaware Art Museum?

A. Edward Loper Jr.

Q. Where in Delaware can one see a collection of Campbell Soup tureens?

A. Winterthur Museum.

Q. Ghosts, goblins, and other supernatural phenomena in Delmarva are subjects for a series of books by what Newark-based author?

A. Ed Okonowicz.

Q. The familiar initials in N. C. Wyeth's name stand for what?

A. Newell Convers.

Q. What contemporary Delaware artist seeks spiritual inspiration in her paintings of children, sand dunes, and the wonders of life?

A. Carolyn Blish.

Q. What memorial to the wife of General J. Ernest Smith is the site of the Brandywine Arts Festival?

A. Josephine Garden.

Q. What was Wilmington's first morning newspaper, started in 1876?

A. The *Morning Herald*.

Q. Which Delawarean wrote the 1926 novel *Demigods*?

A. Judge John Biggs.

Q. What is the name of the student newspaper at Saint Andrew's School near Middletown?

A. The *Cardinal*.

Q. "The Milford Bard" referred to what nineteenth-century physician, writer, and poet?

A. John Lofland.

Q. Where in Wilmington is the New Castle County Law Library located?

A. Daniel Herrmann Courthouse.

Q. The eighteenth-century painter Charles Willson Peale was first taught by what Delaware artist?

A. John Hesselius.

Q. The *Saturday Review of Literature* was founded by what Delaware native in 1924?

A. Henry S. Canby.

Q. Who wrote *The Great Delaware Sports Book*, published in 1995?

A. Doug Gelbert.

Q. Which local writer penned a book about Wilmington as the nation's corporate capital in the twentieth century?

A. Carol E. Hoffecker.

Q. Seventeenth-century antiques are among the furnishings in what New Castle dwelling thought to be the oldest brick house in the state?

A. Old Dutch House.

Q. Who was the African-American teacher and writer who founded the *Advocate* in Wilmington in the 1920s?

A. Alice Dunbar Nelson.

Q. Benjamin Ferris, who died in 1867, was the author of what book?

A. *A History of the Original Settlements on the Delaware.*

Q. What is the name of the Greenville-based novelist who writes about World War I veteran and Scotland Yard detective Ian Rutledge?

A. Charles Todd.

Q. Who wrote the book, *Towarzystwo Czytelni Polskiej, 1898–1998*, about the centenary of the Polish Library Association in Wilmington?

A. Thomas Duszak.

Q. *Notes from the Shore* was written by which Sussex County author?

A. Jennifer Ackerman.

Q. Who sculpted the bronze-and-stone Holocaust monument next to the Delaware State Building in Wilmington?

A. Elbert Weinberg.

———∞∞∞———

Q. Who painted the monumental mural inside the main entrance of the Wilmington Trust Center on Rodney Square North?

A. Elizabeth Abrams Thompson.

———∞∞∞———

Q. What Delaware native and *National Geographic* photographer is responsible for the 1992 book *Delaware Discovered*?

A. Kevin Fleming.

———∞∞∞———

Q. The Delaware Division of the Arts hosts revolving art shows in a mezzanine gallery of what tall downtown Wilmington structure?

A. Carvel State Building.

———∞∞∞———

Q. What Delaware poet laureate, born in 1890, was commissioned to write a poem for the 1951 dedication of the Delaware Memorial Bridge?

A. Jeannette Slocomb Edwards.

———∞∞∞———

Q. What is believed to have been Delaware's first newspaper, published in 1760?

A. The *Wilmington Chronicle*.

Q. Where in Delaware can visitors see the largest collection of late nineteenth-century pre-Raphaelite art on display in the United States?

A. Delaware Art Museum.

Q. What nineteenth-century architect designed Wilmington's stylish Baltimore and Ohio and Pennsylvania Railroad stations?

A. Frank Furness.

Q. Who wrote a history of the Fenwick Island Lighthouse, which was completed in 1859 and decommissioned in 1978?

A. Dorothy Pepper of Selbyville.

Q. What shipping company in 1887 was the first Wilmington business to have an office typewriter?

A. Warner Company.

Q. Who was the first woman doctor in Delaware, a pediatrician who founded the Mothers Milk Bank in the 1940s?

A. Dr. Margaret I. Handy.

Q. What Delaware teacher and scholar wrote *Colonial Delaware: A History*, published in 1978?

A. John A. Munroe.

Q. What object left overnight do storytellers say will summon the ghost of the prominent eighteenth-century farmer who built the governor's mansion?

A. A glass of sherry.

Q. From what source did designers of the Delaware flag take the colors buff and blue?

A. George Washington's uniform.

Q. For how many years was the *Delaware Gazette* newspaper published?

A. Ninety-seven (1785–1882).

Q. Famed "urbanologist" William H. Whyte, known for his 1956 best-seller *The Organization Man*, attended which Delaware high school?

A. Saint Andrew's.

Q. The University of Delaware has a significant collection of items representing what form of Russian religious art?

A. Icons.

Q. Who wrote the music for the state song?

A. Will M. S. Brown.

Q. The Delaware College of Art and Design initially offered what degree?

A. Fine Arts Associate.

Q. The oil painting of John Dickinson, now on display in Delaware Chancery Court, is the work of what twentieth-century artist?

A. Ethel P. B. Leach.

Q. The lyrics of the Delaware state song were written by what two people?

A. George B. Hynson and Donn Devine.

Q. Which member of the du Pont family originally owned the estate now occupied by the Winterthur Museum?

A. Henry Francis du Pont.

Q. Wilmington's earliest library is believed to have been founded in what year?

A. 1754.

Q. The subject of Hal Roth's recent book *The Monster's Handsome Face* is what notorious nineteenth-century woman?

A. Patty Cannon.

Q. What antislavery newspaper was founded in 1854 by Delawarean Mary Ann Shadd Cary?

A. The *Provincial Freedman.*

Q. In which library can scholars locate oral histories of workers from the du Pont powder mills?

A. Hagley Museum.

Q. Who wrote the controversial 1974 book *DuPont: Behind the Nylon Curtain*?

A. Gerard Zilg.

Q. For what novel did Wilmington-born John P. Marquand receive the Pulitzer Prize for fiction?

A. *The Late George Apley.*

Q. Visitors to Delaware Art Museum enjoy Pre-Raphaelite art that was once in the collection of which Wilmington business family?

A. Bancroft.

Q. The state's digital library, accessed through the World Wide Web at www.lib.de.us, has what name?

A. DelAWARE.

Q. Photographer Fred Comegys's pictorial tour of the state, published in 1988, has what name?

A. *Delaware: Close to Home.*

———— ∞ ————

Q. What nineteenth-century Delaware playwright found success in New York with his antislavery play *The Gladiator*?

A. Robert Montgomery Bird.

———— ∞ ————

Q. The University of Delaware is the repository of books, letters, pictures, reviews, and assorted memorabilia of what nineteenth-century British poet?

A. Lord Byron.

———— ∞ ————

Q. What physical artifact is part of the Lord Byron Society collection at the University of Delaware?

A. A strand of his hair.

———— ∞ ————

Q. Adolf Hitler's cinematographer, Leni Riefenstahl, was the subject of a work by what Wilmington playwright?

A. David Robson.

———— ∞ ————

Q. The writer Upton Sinclair was once a resident of what artsy "single tax" village?

A. Arden.

SPORTS & LEISURE

C H A P T E R   F I V E

Q. What state track is used for professional NASCAR auto racing?

A. Dover Downs (International Speedway).

—⊗⊗⊗—

Q. For more than thirty years Cape Henlopen has been the scene of what annual spring event, with strings attached?

A. The Great Delaware Kite Festival.

—⊗⊗⊗—

Q. What name was given to Delaware's minor league baseball team?

A. Wilmington Blue Rocks.

—⊗⊗⊗—

Q. Members of the Delaware Wizards play what sport?

A. Soccer.

—⊗⊗⊗—

Q. Who was the celebrated Wimbledon women's doubles tennis champion who played for the Delaware Smash in the summer of 2000?

A. Serena Williams.

Q. What professional heavyweight boxer lived and trained in Elsmere and fought Evander Holyfield in 1998 at the Georgia Dome?

A. Vaughn Bean.

Q. How many miles of hiking trails cover White Clay Creek State Park?

A. Twenty.

Q. What is the nickname for the University of Delaware's football team?

A. The Blue Hens.

Q. The DuPont Country Club annually hosts what national championship event?

A. LPGA (Ladies Professional Golfing Association).

Q. Where is thoroughbred horse racing held in northern Delaware?

A. Delaware Park.

Q. Each spring Winterthur Museum hosts what popular sports and social event?

A. Point-to-Point.

Q. On what date is the First Night Dover celebration held?

A. December 31.

———∞∞∞———

Q. Where do the Blue Rocks play baseball in Delaware?

A. Frawley Stadium, Wilmington.

———∞∞∞———

Q. What former *News-Journal* sportswriter, editor, and walking encyclopedia for many years wrote the column "A La Carte"?

A. Al Cartwright.

———∞∞∞———

Q. In the early part of the twentieth century, what popular amusement park was situated west of Wilmington?

A. Brandywine Springs.

———∞∞∞———

Q. What Princeton-educated Delaware resident periodically works part-time as a prizefighter?

A. Henry Milligan.

———∞∞∞———

Q. What John Dickinson High School grad played for the Nashville Predators in 1999–2000?

A. Mark Eaton.

Q. In 1969 who won the first NASCAR-sanctioned race at Dover Downs?

A. Richard Petty.

Q. What is the modified Delaware version of the famous Boston footrace?

A. Caesar Rodney Half Marathon.

Q. Which Delaware financial firm sponsors an annual Winston Cup NASCAR event at Dover Downs Speedway?

A. MBNA bank.

Q. What are the University of Delaware's colors?

A. Blue and Gold.

Q. What was the name of the internationally recognized bicycle race sponsored in the early 1990s by a Delaware company?

A. Tour du Pont.

Q. Which auto racing group returned to Dover Downs International Speedway in 1998 after an almost thirty-year hiatus?

A. Indy Racing League.

Q. How many parking meters does Rehoboth Beach have available for visitors?

A. 2,200.

Q. What distance does a single lap cover at Dover Downs?

A. One mile.

———

Q. What Wilmington man played for the Philadelphia Phillies in both Connie Mack Stadium and Veterans Stadium?

A. Organist Paul Richardson.

———

Q. How many laps do race car drivers complete at Dover Downs in a 400K race?

A. Around 250.

———

Q. Christ Church, Christiana Hundred, hosts what charity event each winter?

A. Green Show.

———

Q. Who founded wrestling as a legitimate sport in Delaware schools, in 1931?

A. William Cameron of Saint Andrews.

———

Q. In 1998 what aquatic feat did eleven-year-old Dayna Peden of New Castle accomplish?

A. She swam the Delaware River.

———

Q. What modern-day professional pugilist trained in a farmhouse off Centerville Road in Greenville?

A. Michael Spinks.

Q. Cape Henlopen State Park covers how many acres?

A. Four thousand.

Q. How many spectator seats are at Dover Downs?

A. Around one hundred thousand.

Q. Which two winning race car drivers had fathers who also won races at Dover Downs?

A. Davey Allison and Kyle Petty.

Q. Who won the LPGA championship in Delaware in 1993 and in 1994?

A. Laura Davies.

Q. Before becoming a football star with the Dallas Cowboys in the 1970s and 1980s, Randy White attended what Delaware high school?

A. McKean.

Q. What professional boxing promoter owned a house near Greenville?

A. Butch Lewis.

Q. Where do Olympic hopefuls and amateurs ice skate at the University of Delaware?

A. Blue and Gold Ice Arenas.

Q. What is the average speed of an Indy racing car at Dover Downs?

A. Around ninety-nine miles per hour.

———— ∞ ————

Q. Amateur-league softball diamonds at the DuPont Company Experimental Station are next to which park in New Castle County?

A. Alapocas Woods.

———— ∞ ————

Q. In Delaware what is the standard legal minimum driving age?

A. Eighteen.

———— ∞ ————

Q. At what annual event near Millsboro can visitors see Native-American dancing and craft-making?

A. Nanticoke Indian Pow-Wow.

———— ∞ ————

Q. What is the nickname of Wesley College's football team?

A. Wolverines.

———— ∞ ————

Q. How long does it take to complete a 400K race at Dover's professional auto speedway?

A. Approximately two and one-half hours.

———— ∞ ————

Q. Professional race car drivers gave what nickname to Dover Downs?

A. Monster Mile.

Q. When was the Delaware Pushmobile Derby founded?

A. 1929.

———⊗———

Q. What Delaware track-and-field star ran the steeplechase in the 1964 Tokyo Olympics?

A. Vic Zwolak.

———⊗———

Q. When did the "Old Blue Rocks" stop playing professional baseball in Wilmington?

A. 1952.

———⊗———

Q. What scenic state park is located on the Delaware River at Edgemoor?

A. Fox Point.

———⊗———

Q. What is the name of the narrow sloping parkland that leads from Trolley Square to the Brandywine?

A. Rattlesnake Run.

———⊗———

Q. Which two Phillies "whiz kids" played baseball for the original Wilmington Blue Rocks early in their careers?

A. Robin Roberts and Curt Simmons.

———⊗———

Q. Just after the Civil War, what team sport became increasingly popular with the youth of Wilmington?

A. Baseball.

Q. What rowing competition is held annually near Middletown?

A. Diamond State Regatta.

———∞∞∞———

Q. The ever-growing June carnival held by a West Wilmington Roman Catholic Church is known by what name?

A. Saint Anthony's Italian Festival.

———∞∞∞———

Q. Founded in 1883, what was the first short-lived professional baseball team in Wilmington?

A. Quicksteps.

———∞∞∞———

Q. What sport does the glitzy museum, theme restaurant, and showroom at Interstate 295 and New Castle Avenue memorialize?

A. Harley Davidson motorcyle riding.

———∞∞∞———

Q. What is the seating capacity of the University of Delaware football stadium?

A. Approximately twenty-three thousand.

———∞∞∞———

Q. Which northern Delaware state park holds a Sledding Festival after the first big snowfall of the winter season?

A. Brandywine Creek.

———∞∞∞———

Q. Baseball games in the late 1800s took place at the old "ball grounds" near what West Side Wilmington intersection?

A. Front and Union Streets.

Q. Where is the annual Diamond State Regatta held?

A. Noxontown Pond.

Q. Wilmington officials at the turn of the twenty-first century envisioned what sort of sports facility in Rodney Square?

A. Ice rink.

Q. About how much money did professional baseball players earn weekly in Wilmington in the late 1880s?

A. Forty dollars.

Q. What material made up the road surface of Dover Downs auto raceway?

A. Concrete.

Q. In what sport did members of the Wilmington Powder Monkeys participate in the nineteenth century?

A. Baseball.

Q. The Governor's Cup at the annual Delaware State Fair is awarded in what sport?

A. Harness racing.

Q. What winning boys' football team in Delaware participates only in "home" games?

A. Ferris School.

Q. In what sport do the Delmarva Destroyers participate?

A. Football.

———⊗———

Q. What track and football field is maintained by the state parks department on West Eighteenth Street in Wilmington?

A. Baynard Stadium.

———⊗———

Q. In 1976 Delaware was designated as the eastern touchdown point of which cross-country women's airplane race?

A. Powder Puff Derby.

———⊗———

Q. Who was the 1960s pitcher from Georgetown who became a Philadelphia Phillies star?

A. Chris Short.

———⊗———

Q. What was the record qualifying speed set by Indy racer Tony Stuart at Dover Downs speedway in 1998?

A. 185.2 miles per hour.

———⊗———

Q. What heavyweight champ sometimes coaches boxers in Elsmere?

A. Joe Frazier.

———⊗———

Q. How many clams may be legally harvested by state residents daily, in designated areas, without a permit?

A. One hundred.

Q. Who sponsors the annual children's Delaware Pushmobile Derby race?

A. Delaware Association of Police.

Q. The Blue Rocks minor-league baseball team is affiliated with what major-league team?

A. Kansas City Royals.

Q. The Wilmington Blue Rocks belong to which of baseball's minor leagues?

A. Carolina.

Q. Delaware surfers ride their boards in competition at what Atlantic shore inlet?

A. Indian River.

Q. What Ukrainian woman figure skater, a 1994 Olympic gold medal winner, trained at the University of Delaware ice arenas?

A. Oksana Baiul.

Q. What University of Delaware baseball star went on to lead the Philadelphia Phillies to a world championship in 1980?

A. Dallas Green.

Q. Sussex County Airport, the largest paved airfield in lower Delaware, is near which city?

A. Georgetown.

Q. Martina Navratilova, with nineteen Wimbledon titles, played for the Delaware Smash in what years?

A. 1996 to 1998.

Q. Later a police officer, Sophia Hunter-Sheppard excelled at what sport at Delaware State University in the mid-1980s?

A. Track.

Q. William Julius Johnson, a baseball Hall of Famer from Wilmington who played in the former Negro Leagues of the 1920s and 1930s, had what nickname?

A. Judy.

Q. What is the name of the tasty clawed shellfish harvested from Delaware Bay?

A. Blue Crabs.

Q. At what state park do Delaware model aircraft flyers practice their sport?

A. Lums Pond.

Q. What aerial sport is represented annually in a festival near Milton?

A. Hot-air ballooning.

———❦———

Q. How many golf courses are located in Sussex County?

A. Fifteen.

———❦———

Q. The "Old Blue Rocks" served as a farm team for what two major league teams?

A. Phillies and Athletics.

———❦———

Q. In 1946 star athlete Gerald "Doc" Doherty III helped the University of Delaware to titles in what two sports?

A. Football and baseball.

———❦———

Q. In the summer Brandywine Creek is the place to go for what two leisure sports for families?

A. Tubing and canoeing.

———❦———

Q. Ron Waller of Laurel played for what professional football team during the 1950s?

A. The Rams.

———❦———

Q. Where in New Castle County is the annual Ice Cream Festival held?

A. Rockwood Museum.

Q. The Delaware State University football team is known by what nickname?

A. Hornets.

Q. On which three Delaware ponds may boats be rented from the state?

A. Lums, Killens, and Trap.

Q. Where is Delaware's only thirty-six-hole golf course?

A. DuPont Country Club.

Q. Designated camping facilities are available at what five state parks?

A. Cape Henlopen, Seashore, and Trap, Killens, and Lums Ponds.

Q. Delaware law requires waterfowl hunters to use what type of environmentally safe ammunition?

A. Steel shot.

Q. Daniel Frawley, for whom Frawley Stadium was named, held what public office in Wilmington?

A. Mayor.

Q. Which all-time tennis great founded World Team Tennis in the 1970s and owns half of the Delaware Smash?

A. Billie Jean King.

Q. Before World War II, the Delaware State Fair was held in what town?

A. Elsmere.

Q. The Wilmington Colts play what high-school-level sport?

A. Rugby.

Q. Dionna Harris, 1996 Delaware Sportswriters and Broadcasters Association Athlete of the Year and Olympic gold medalist, excelled at what sport?

A. Softball.

Q. What Delaware professional golfer won the 1993 Women's Open?

A. Laurie Merten.

Q. How many artificial reefs have been placed off the Delaware shore to attract fish?

A. Eleven.

Q. Delino DeShields of Seaford, a member of four professional teams in the 1990s, plays what sport?

A. Baseball.

Q. What is the name of the riding academy at Bellevue State Park?

A. Wellspring Farm.

Q. In what football conference do the Delaware State University Hornets play?

A. Mid-Eastern Athletic.

Q. Which two non-tidal ponds in Delaware provide wheelchair access for fishing?

A. Records and Logan Lane.

Q. In what year was the Delaware Sports Hall of Fame started?

A. 1976.

Q. Hunters may shoot clay pigeons and take hunting safety courses at what River Road facility south of New Castle?

A. Ommelanden Range.

Q. Wilmingtonian Brett Lunger excelled in what internationally recognized sport?

A. Auto racing.

Q. When are thoroughbred horseracing events held live at Delaware Park, Stanton?

A. April–November.

Q. In what city is Delaware's only U.S. military golf course situated?

A. Dover.

Q. At what age is a license required to fish in Delaware?

A. Sixteen.

Q. In what year did Dover Downs open?

A. 1969.

Q. Dave Nelson coached what sport at the University of Delaware?

A. Football.

Q. Where are the two best spots for taking crabs and clams in Delaware?

A. Along Indian River and Rehoboth Bay.

Q. What tourist destination in the Delaware River is accessible only by boat from Delaware City?

A. Fort Delaware.

Q. The Wilmington Blue Bombers played basketball in the 1960s in what gym?

A. Salesianum School.

Q. The grassy public area in the middle of historic Old New Castle has what name?

A. The Green.

Q. The Delaware Blue Bombers started playing in what year?

A. 1993.

Q. What promising Delaware middleweight prizefighter retired in his twenties to do community work after a points squabble in 1992?

A. Dave Tiberi.

Q. Delaware Sports Hall of Famer Bunny Vosters played what sport?

A. Tennis.

Q. In which football conference does Wesley College play?

A. Atlantic Central.

Q. After World War II, what four small southern Delaware cities had active minor-league baseball teams?

A. Dover, Milford, Seaford, and Rehoboth.

Q. What African-American baseball team was transplanted from Washington, D.C., to Delaware in 1925?

A. Wilmington Potomacs.

Q. R. R. M. Carpenter of Greenville bought what professional baseball team in the 1940s?

A. Philadelphia Phillies.

Q. What kind of fish can be caught in September, October, and November by bottom fishing around Delaware's ocean wrecks and artificial reefs?

A. Tautog.

———⁂———

Q. To be legally licensed to hunt in Delaware, anyone born in or after 1967 must pass what course?

A. Hunter education.

———⁂———

Q. William du Pont Jr., one of the state's best-known horse owners, designed what racetrack?

A. Delaware Park.

———⁂———

Q. What Wilmington public golf course bears the name of a well-known golf pro?

A. Ed "Porky" Oliver.

———⁂———

Q. Dover Downs, Harrington Raceway, and Delaware Park supplemented racing with what new form of entertainment in the 1990s?

A. Slot machines.

———⁂———

Q. How much money did Jeff Gordon win driving a DuPont Company sponsored race car in NASCAR's 1998 Brickyard 400?

A. $1.63 million.

Q. Concord High School's Vicki Huber ran in the Olympics at Seoul, Korea, and was featured in *Sports Illustrated* in what year?

A. 1988.

Q. The Wilmington Wildcats Club sponsors sessions in what sport?

A. Wrestling.

Q. What ponds in Kent and Sussex Counties are designated for seasonal stocking of trout?

A. Tidbury and Gravel Hill.

Q. For what sport was World War II–era Delaware sports hero Al Tribuani famous?

A. Boxing.

Q. How much must a freshwater striped bass weigh to be kept by Delaware anglers?

A. At least twenty pounds.

Q. What central public park in Dover is used for swimming, fishing, boating, and jogging?

A. Silver Lake.

Q. Bicycle racer Greg LeMond won the Tour du Pont in what year?

A. 1992.

———∞∞∞———

Q. What Wilmington city councilman and radio personality started a youth basketball league in the 1980s?

A. "Stormin' " Norman Oliver.

———∞∞∞———

Q. What game resembling bowling do men of Italian extraction play in Saint Anthony's Parish, Wilmington?

A. Bocci.

———∞∞∞———

Q. What species of fish may legally be caught in Delaware with a bow and arrow?

A. Carp.

———∞∞∞———

Q. Who coached the University of Delaware men's tennis team for a record forty years (1953–1993)?

A. Dr. Roy Rylander.

———∞∞∞———

Q. Who was Delaware State's "Red Bandit," a star basketball player in 1980 and later a tax accountant?

A. Anthony Baylor.

———∞∞∞———

Q. Bombay Hook National Wildlife Refuge southeast of Smyrna covers how many square miles?

A. Twenty-three.

Q. In Kent County, people board "head boats" at Bowers Beach for what popular sport?

A. Deep-sea fishing.

———❧———

Q. What Native-American artifact repository is situated near Millsboro?

A. Nanticoke Indian Museum.

———❧———

Q. How many trout are anglers allowed to catch daily in Delaware?

A. Six.

———❧———

Q. What museum in Lewes honors the original Dutch settlers?

A. Zwaanendael.

———❧———

Q. What nonprofit group develops nature trails and promotes wildlife education along rural Sussex County waterways?

A. Center for the Inland Bays.

———❧———

Q. March and April are the best months for catching what species of fish just offshore?

A. Atlantic mackerel.

———❧———

Q. Sport pilots can land at how many public airports with grass runways?

A. Four.

Q. The tasty Delaware Bay weakfish is known by what nickname?

A. Sea trout.

Q. What is the maximum number of rods a person may use while fishing in the state's nontidal waters?

A. Two.

Q. In what event did Delawarean Frank Masley compete during three Winter Olympic events in the 1980s?

A. Luge.

Q. What official enforces Delaware's strict 1993 code governing bungee jumping?

A. State fire marshal.

Q. What high jumper at the 1972 Munich Olympics attended Newark High School and Colgate University, then became a psychologist?

A. Chris Dunn.

Q. A designated parachute jumping area is defined on U.S. aviation charts near what Delaware airfield?

A. Laurel.

Q. The Wilmington Blue Rocks won Carolina League championships in what years?

A. 1994, 1996, and 1998.

Q. Dover's Frank Shakespeare won an Olympic gold medal at Helsinki in 1952 in what sport?

A. Rowing.

Q. Undersea canyons off the Delaware coast are prime summer trolling areas for what two game fish?

A. White marlin and yellowfin tuna.

Q. During World War I, what baseball legend worked for Wilmington's Harlan and Hollingsworth shipyard?

A. Shoeless Joe Jackson.

Q. In what sport did 1972 Olympic gold medalist Frank Shorter of Delaware participate?

A. Marathon.

Q. What baseball pitching star and Hall of Famer managed the Wilmington Blue Rocks in 1940?

A. Chief Bender.

Q. How does the state use the money paid for fishing licenses?

A. Fish conservation.

Q. In what year did the Delaware Sportswriters and Broadcasters Association begin selecting Delaware's Athletes of the Year?

A. 1949.

Q. The legendary head football coach for the University of Delaware, Harold R. Raymond, is known by what nickname?

A. Tubby.

Q. On what private estate in New Castle County can visitors tour a maze garden?

A. Nemours.

Q. In two manifestations during the twentieth century, a Wilmington professional football team took what name?

A. Clippers.

Q. Which Delaware city produced a national championship boys' senior Little League baseball team in 1981?

A. Georgetown.

Q. What variety of hooks do Delaware fish and wildlife officials recommend for live-release fishing?

A. Barbless.

Q. Controlled hunting in what deer-overpopulated northern state park is permitted periodically?

A. Brandywine Creek.

Q. How many seats are in the Bob Carpenter Center at the University of Delaware?

A. 5,058.

———∞———

Q. What Delaware woman, once a professional bowling champion, became a New Castle County executive?

A. Rita Justice.

———∞———

Q. Which upscale Wilmington neighborhood was used in the early 1900s as a track for horseracing?

A. Wawaset Park.

———∞———

Q. In what year did Delaware begin legalizing slot machines at its major racetracks?

A. 1995.

———∞———

Q. Allaire du Pont of Delaware, widow of Richard du Pont, owned what legendary race horse of the 1960s?

A. Kelso.

———∞———

Q. In 1993 what *News-Journal* sportswriter was inducted into the Delaware Sports Hall of Fame?

A. Izzy Katzman.

Q. Scup, the saltwater game fish found on the Delaware coast, is known by what other name?

A. Porgy.

Q. What *Wilmington News Journal* reporter with a last name beginning with Z writes about local sports figures?

A. Matt Zabitka

Q. In how many NCAA playoffs did the University of Delaware football team take part during the 1990s?

A. Six.

Q. What scenic wooded tract is situated west of U.S. 13 between Townsend and Clayton?

A. Blackbird State Forest.

Q. Legendary University of Delaware football coaches Dave Nelson and Tubby Raymond both attended which college?

A. University of Michigan.

Q. Ed Koffenberger was named to the Delaware Sports Hall of Fame in 1977 for excellence in what sport?

A. Basketball.

Q. Where can bungee jumpers legally practice their sport in Delaware?

A. Nowhere.

SCIENCE & NATURE

CHAPTER SIX

Q. The nine-eyed *Limulus polyphemus*, which lives in Delaware Bay and lays eggs on the Kent County shoreline, is known by what popular name?

A. Horseshoe crab.

———— ◇◇◇ ————

Q. How many fresh-water lakes are found in Delaware?

A. Around fifty.

———— ◇◇◇ ————

Q. What DuPont Company scientist discovered nylon in the 1930s?

A. Dr. Wallace H. Carothers.

———— ◇◇◇ ————

Q. Delaware has more people per capita with what scientific academic degree than any other state?

A. Ph.D.

———— ◇◇◇ ————

Q. Where are the three Federal Aviation Administration electronic navigational aids for pilots in Delaware?

A. New Castle, Smyrna, and Broadkill Beach.

Q. Before the DuPont Company gave the world nylon, what two materials were used to make ladies stockings?

A. Silk and cotton.

———— ∞ ————

Q. Why was nylon hosiery extremely scarce during World War II?

A. Nylon was needed for parachutes.

———— ∞ ————

Q. Where does Delaware rank among the states in per capita receipt of patent awards?

A. First.

———— ∞ ————

Q. The DuPont Company built its Seaford Plant to make what product?

A. Nylon.

———— ∞ ————

Q. The state's only oil refinery is situated just north of what community?

A. Delaware City.

———— ∞ ————

Q. How many nuclear generators are located at the Salem reactor facility on Artificial Island in the Delaware River?

A. Three.

Q. What is the term for the boundary between the fresh water from the upper Delaware River and tidal sea water moving in from the Atlantic?

A. Salt line.

Q. How long is the longest runway at Dover Air Force Base?

A. 12,900 feet.

Q. What whitening product does the DuPont Company make at the Edgemoor plant?

A. Titanium dioxide.

Q. Which two automobile companies have assembly plants in Delaware?

A. GM and DaimlerChrysler.

Q. What is Delaware's only known poisonous snake, which is found along the Brandywine River?

A. Copperhead.

Q. Where near Newark can visitors see exhibits on Delaware wildlife, fossils, minerals, and prehistoric artifacts?

A. Iron Hill Museum.

Q. What delicacy favored in Asia is available by fishing in the Christina River?

A. Eels.

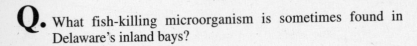

Q. What fish-killing microorganism is sometimes found in Delaware's inland bays?

A. *Pfiesteria piscicida.*

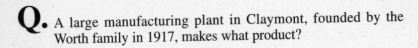

Q. A large manufacturing plant in Claymont, founded by the Worth family in 1917, makes what product?

A. Steel.

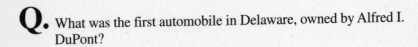

Q. What was the first automobile in Delaware, owned by Alfred I. DuPont?

A. 1897 Benz.

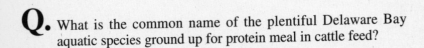

Q. What is the common name of the plentiful Delaware Bay aquatic species ground up for protein meal in cattle feed?

A. Menhaden.

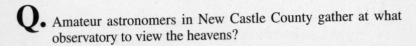

Q. Amateur astronomers in New Castle County gather at what observatory to view the heavens?

A. Mount Cuba.

Q. When does the University of Delaware College of Marine Studies host Coast Day at the Lewes campus?

A. First Sunday in October.

Q. Where does Wilmington get the water it stores in Hoope's Reservoir?

A. Brandywine River.

Q. During the 1940s the U.S. government performed secret rocket testing at what site in Delaware?

A. Dover Army Airfield.

Q. According to Delaware wildlife officials, how many beaver colonies are in the state?

A. Approximately 260.

Q. New Castle County contains how many miles of sanitary sewer lines?

A. 1,540.

Q. What Wilmington-based company has positioned itself to become the world's largest auto paint supplier?

A. DuPont.

Q. The statewide firm that started out in 1905 as the Richardson Park Water Company now has what name?

A. Artesian.

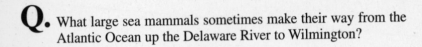

Q. What large sea mammals sometimes make their way from the Atlantic Ocean up the Delaware River to Wilmington?

A. Whales.

Q. In what year did Delaware begin using voting machines instead of paper ballots?

A. 1954.

Q. Bullet-resistant vests for police are made of what DuPont Company fiber product?

A. Kevlar.

Q. On the banks of what waterway in Delaware can fossils of the Cretaceous period be found?

A. The Chesapeake and Delaware Canal.

Q. What is Delaware's state flower?

A. Peach blossom.

Q. The DuPont Company first developed silicon at what site?

A. Newport.

Q. What Delaware nonprofit organization is involved with research into and rehabilitation of oiled or injured winged wildlife?

A. Tri-state Bird Rescue.

Q. What kind of business along the Brandywine, started by Oliver Canby in 1752, helped make Wilmington a major trade center?

A. Flour mill.

Q. Which global pharmaceutical firm has its North American headquarters in Fairfax?

A. Astra Zeneca.

Q. Where is the natural habitat of the Brandywine Zoo's tigers?

A. Siberia.

Q. Delaware's Protein Technology International, Inc., uses what heart-healthy raw material to make its product?

A. Soybeans.

Q. Local doctors and dentists founded what organization in 1930 to foster interest in medicine, science, and education?

A. Delaware Academy of Medicine.

Q. How many full-sized buses can fit inside a C-5 cargo plane at Dover Air Force Base?

A. Six.

Q. Brandywine Mills, founded by Joseph Bancroft in the 1800s, processed what material?

A. Cotton.

Q. Automobiles often have 14, 15, or 16-inch wheels, but Delaware Dart bus wheels are how many inches in diameter?

A. Twenty-two and a half.

Q. Penny Hall at the University of Delaware contains a comprehensive collection of what items from around the world?

A. Gems and minerals.

Q. In the late 1700s, Joshua and Thomas Gilpin opened what type of milling operation on the Brandywine?

A. Paper.

Q. What is the average winter temperature for Delaware?

A. Thirty-three degrees Fahrenheit.

Q. What state agency monitors subterranean tremors and plots the intensity and location of earthquakes?

A. Delaware Geological Survey.

Q. What is the largest civil aircraft that has landed at New Castle County Airport?

A. Air Force One.

Q. In the early 1800s what was the primary chemical product produced by the new DuPont Company along the Brandywine?

A. Gunpowder.

Q. Nancy Decker Currie, who grew up near Wilmington, made what career choice?

A. Astronaut.

Q. What was the name of Delaware's first aircraft, flown in 1910 at Wawaset Park?

A. Delaplane.

Q. On display at the Brandywine Zoo are what large South American birds?

A. Andean condors.

Q. What is the only civilian airfield in Delaware with an FAA Air Traffic Control tower?

A. New Castle County Airport.

Q. Historic weather data for all of Delaware is collected and analyzed by what official?

A. The state climatologist.

Q. Each year, which endangered species of bird nests on sandy Cape Henlopen?

A. Piping plover.

Q. What was the name of the pioneering French scientist who tutored Irenee du Pont in chemistry?

A. Antoine Lavoisier.

Q. How many gems and minerals are on display at the Irenee du Pont Mineral Room in Penny Hall at the University of Delaware?

A. Approximately six thousand.

Q. The DuPont Company's presence inspired what nickname for Wilmington?

A. Chemical Capital of the World.

Q. Scientists suggested controlling alfalfa-destroying bugs in Kent County by introducing what tiny European insects?

A. Stingless wasps.

Q. What is Delaware's state tree?

A. American holly.

Q. Dr. Henry Heimlich, inventor of the life-saving Heimlich maneuver, was born in what city?

A. Wilmington.

Q. A fiery meteorite is said to have landed near which Sussex County town in 1887?

A. Millville.

Q. What three nuclear power plants are on Artificial Island?

A. Salem I, Salem II, and Hope Creek.

Q. *Porthetria dispar*, an insect that periodically ravishes tree foliage in Delaware, is popularly called by what name?

A. Gypsy moth.

Q. ILC Dover, Inc., manufactures what major product for the National Aeronautics and Space Administration?

A. Space suits.

Q. Which Delaware military unit provided short-haul cargo service for the Persian Gulf War of 1991?

A. Air National Guard.

Q. When the Delaware Memorial Bridge opened in 1951, how did it rate in length among suspension bridges in the world?

A. Sixth.

Q. Delaware is the largest importer in the United States of what beverage shipped in sea tankers?

A. Orange juice concentrate.

Q. The botanical miracle found growing in Delaware Seashore State Park after a hundred-year hiatus has what common name?

A. Amaranth.

Q. How many miles of tidal shoreline does Delaware have?

A. 381.

———— ∞ ————

Q. How does Delaware rank among the "lowest" states, with its land lying closest to sea level?

A. Second (only Florida is lower).

———— ∞ ————

Q. Who founded a Kent County dental supply manufacturing plant in his Camden kitchen in 1877?

A. Dr. Levin C. Caulk.

———— ∞ ————

Q. What primary commodity available from Native Americans attracted the Swedes to Delaware in the early 1600s?

A. Beaver pelts.

———— ∞ ————

Q. What kind of cargo aircraft did the Delaware Air National Guard fly in Iraq in 1991?

A. C-130s.

———— ∞ ————

Q. Owners of nonnative snakes must pay how much money to obtain an exotic pet license from the state?

A. $25.

Q. Recycling rags in Brandywine mills in the nineteenth century caused masses of what items to be dumped in nearby fields?

A. Buttons.

———⌾∞⌾———

Q. The African-American and Irish laborers who dug the Chesapeake and Delaware Canal in the early 1800s faced what major health peril?

A. Malaria.

———⌾∞⌾———

Q. Delaware's poultry industry began by accident in 1923 when what resident of Ocean View ordered fifty chicks and received five hundred instead?

A. Cecile Steele.

———⌾∞⌾———

Q. Delaware's state fish, *Cynoscion regalis*, goes by what popular name?

A. Weakfish.

———⌾∞⌾———

Q. The Chesapeake and Delaware Canal gives the state what unique geographic distinction among the other states?

A. It is the only state completely bisected by a sea-level canal.

———⌾∞⌾———

Q. In data collected since 1948, a record of 12.6 inches of rain fell in Wilmington during July of what year?

A. 1989.

Q. Which two fruit crops dominated Delaware agriculture in much of the nineteenth century?

A. Peaches and strawberries.

⸺⸙⸺

Q. What animal is the primary carrier of rabies in Delaware?

A. Raccoon.

⸺⸙⸺

Q. When did engineers finish the second span of the Delaware Memorial Bridges?

A. 1968.

⸺⸙⸺

Q. Wildlife exhibits from around the world and a look at Australia's Great Barrier Reef are on display at what Kennett Pike facility?

A. Delaware Museum of Natural History.

⸺⸙⸺

Q. Situated in Wilmington, what is Delaware's tallest building?

A. Chase Manhattan Centre (twenty-three stories).

⸺⸙⸺

Q. The northernmost stands of bald cypress trees in the United States are thought to be found in what county?

A. Kent.

Q. How many exotic pet licenses does the state issue, mostly for snakes, every year?

A. Around one hundred.

———⨀———

Q. Besides sand and gravel, what mineral is mined in Delaware?

A. Compounds of magnesium.

———⨀———

Q. Where is the U.S. military's largest mortuary on the East Coast?

A. Dover Air Force Base.

———⨀———

Q. What were Delaware's blue hen chickens best known for in the 1700s?

A. Cockfighting.

———⨀———

Q. What is the official state mineral?

A. Sillimanite.

———⨀———

Q. Before the Great Depression, what custom-designed automobile was manufactured in Delaware?

A. The DuPont.

Q. A Wilmington factory founded at Ninth and Market Streets in 1866 turned out three million of what dental-related product annually in its heyday?

A. Artificial teeth.

Q. Where are Delaware fire fighters trained to battle blazes under actual conditions?

A. State Fire School near Dover.

Q. What large rodent of South American origin appears to be expanding its habitat in Delmarva marshes?

A. Nutria.

Q. The Delaware Society for the Prevention of Cruelty to Animals was chartered by the Delaware legislature in what year?

A. 1873.

Q. In 1958 what Delaware scientist founded the company that developed the miracle fiber Gore-Tex?

A. Wilbert L. Gore.

Q. What is the official insect of the state of Delaware?

A. Ladybug.

Q. What state animal-care agency does not euthanize homeless dogs and cats but cares for them until a home is found?

A. Delaware Humane Association.

Q. Which Delaware college has the southernmost full-service campus.

A. Delaware Technical and Community College.

Q. Archaeologists say that an unknown number of Nanticoke Indian gravesites, some perhaps two thousand years old, are on which state tract in Sussex County?

A. Thompson Island Preserve.

Q. Who is the University of Delaware professor and astrophysicist who specializes in the study of white dwarf stars?

A. Dr. Harry L. Shipman.

Q. The bullet-resistant material Kevlar was invented in 1965 by which two DuPont Company scientists?

A. Stephanie Kwolek and Paul Morgan.

Q. In the 1800s what unique shallow-draft wooden canal boat was built in a town on Broad Creek near the Nanticoke River?

A. Bethel ram.

Q. In the late 1800s why did Delaware fruit growers switch to other crops?

A. Peach blight.

———⊗⊗⊗———

Q. In the 1880s the Wilmington Oil and Leather Company used the skins of what animal for fine gloves and other waterproof products?

A. Porpoise.

———⊗⊗⊗———

Q. How many miles wide is Delaware at its most narrow point?

A. Nine.

———⊗⊗⊗———

Q. Teflon was discovered by which two DuPont Company scientists?

A. Roy Plunkett and Jack Rebok.

———⊗⊗⊗———

Q. Delaware chicken farmers once added what ingredient to hens' diets to increase calcium intake and produce better eggs?

A. Crushed oyster shells.

———⊗⊗⊗———

Q. A prototype of what high-tech military helicopter-airplane hybrid was assembled and tested in Delaware?

A. Bell-Boeing V-22 Osprey.

Q. From colonial times to the 1940s, what labor-intensive industry was prominent along the Christina River?

A. Shipbuilding.

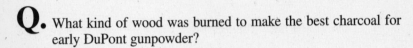

Q. What kind of wood was burned to make the best charcoal for early DuPont gunpowder?

A. Willow.

Q. During World War II members of the Women's Airforce Service Pilots (WASP) trained pilots at and flew "ferry hops" from what Delaware base?

A. New Castle Air Base.

Q. What landmark 1971 law protects the Delaware shoreline from heavy industrialization?

A. Coastal Zone Act.

Q. Delaware chicken farmers keep their incubators at what temperature to hatch eggs?

A. 103 degrees Fahrenheit.

Q. The DuPont Company has given what brand name to its heavy, synthetic, marble-like material that can be drilled, sawed, and sanded?

A. Corian.

Q. How many peach trees were growing in state orchards before 1900?

A. Around eight hundred thousand.

———⊗⊗⊗———

Q. What historic inland structures help Delaware River pilots stay in midchannel?

A. Range lights.

———⊗⊗⊗———

Q. How many different types of aircraft did the Wilmington-based Women's Airforce Service Pilots (WASPs) fly during World War II?

A. Seventy-eight.

———⊗⊗⊗———

Q. In the 1880s Sturgeon packers in Sussex county shipped tons of what commodity?

A. Caviar.

———⊗⊗⊗———

Q. The most harmful natural effect of offshore Atlantic hurricanes and nor'easters in Delaware is what?

A. Beach erosion.

———⊗⊗⊗———

Q. How many wild deer are believed to be on the roam in Delaware?

A. Forty thousand.

Q. The giant C-5 cargo planes at Dover Air Force Base hold how many gallons of fuel each?

A. Around 51,500.

Q. How many feet above mean sea level are the Delaware Memorial Bridge towers?

A. 450.

Q. Which major garment-related industry dominated parts of Wilmington a century ago?

A. Kid leather tanning.

Q. What natural phenomenon is said to have caused heavy damage to Pea Patch Island in the Delaware River in 1846?

A. A tidal wave.

Q. Approximately how many total ship-cargo tons of goods move through the Port of Wilmington annually?

A. 4.5 million.

Q. Where is the Island Field archaeological site with a Native-American burial ground?

A. South Bowers Beach.

Q. Delaware has how many miles of Atlantic Ocean shoreline?

A. Twenty-five.

Q. What old English designation is given to sub-county tracts of land in Delaware?

A. Hundreds.

Q. What renowned aeronautical engineer opened an aircraft factory near New Castle in 1928?

A. Giuseppe Bellanca.

Q. Where is Delaware's cypress swamp located?

A. Near Selbyville.

Q. The DuPont Company sold gunpowder to both sides in what mid-nineteenth-century conflict?

A. Crimean War.

Q. What regional leaf crop first raised by Native Americans was shipped from Delaware to Europe in colonial times?

A. Tobacco.

Q. Delaware was the first state to universally use what high-tech method of recording and counting votes?

A. Electronic voting machines.

Q. What Delaware county produces more broiler chickens than any other county in America?

A. Sussex.

Q. What electrically powered mode of transport do Wilmington planners envision to link the Brandywine and Christina Rivers along Market Street?

A. Trolley.

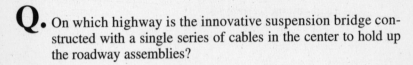

Q. On which highway is the innovative suspension bridge constructed with a single series of cables in the center to hold up the roadway assemblies?

A. Delaware 1 near Saint George's.

Q. In 1941 DuPont Company scientists invented what wool-like acrylic fiber?

A. Orlon.

Q. When did the General Assembly legalize commercial wine-making in Delaware?

A. 1991.

Q. How many miles of rope are used in the rigging of the Wilmington-based *Kalmar Nyckel* ship replica?

A. Six.

Q. What Newport native who created steam powered equipment as early as the late 1700s has been called the "first great American inventor"?

A. Oliver Evans.

Q. How many chickens are produced each year by the state's broiler industry?

A. 255 million.

———— ∞ ————

Q. The three-hundred-year-old, 103-foot-tall red oak tree at Long Neck, near Millsboro, has what nickname?

A. William Penn Oak.

———— ∞ ————

Q. The Brandywine Zoological Gardens gives what name to special weekend activities?

A. Zippity Zoo Days.

———— ∞ ————

Q. The DuPont Company's drug Sustiva is used to combat the effects of what deadly disease?

A. AIDS.

———— ∞ ————

Q. What product did Sussex County woodcutters make from timber harvested in Great Cypress Swamp before a disastrous fire there in 1930?

A. Shingles.

———— ∞ ————

Q. Most of the corn and soybeans grown in Delaware are used for what purpose?

A. Chicken feed.

Q. Mrs. Catherine Fox, who employed commercial trappers on her Delaware Bay marshland before she died in 1936, was known by what nickname?

A. Muskrat Queen of Delaware.

Q. What was the world's first modern divided road, which opened in Delaware in 1933?

A. The DuPont Highway.

Q. After World War II, what U.S. airline set up a major maintenance facility at what is now New Castle County Airport?

A. Trans World Airways.

Q. How many days are in Delaware's standard annual agricultural growing season?

A. Two hundred.

Q. Although temperatures can soar well into the nineties, what is the average summer temperature in Delaware?

A. Seventy-six degrees Fahrenheit.

Q. What company founded by E. R. Johnson manufactured in Dover its product with the famed trademark "His Master's Voice"?

A. Victor Talking Machine Company, maker of the Victrola.

Q. What rare trees brought from China in the 1800s were planted in New Castle?

A. Paulownia.

Q. How many varieties of grapes are grown at Sussex County's Nassau Valley Winery?

A. Seven.

Q. What company with products that include Jell-O, Minute Rice, and Shake-and-Bake operates a factory in Dover?

A. Kraft.

Q. How many licensed aircraft pilots are there in Delaware?

A. 1,750.

Q. Of about eighteen hundred known plant species in Delaware, how many are endangered or disappearing?

A. Almost nine hundred.

Q. Where is the University of Delaware's dairy farm?

A. Newark.

Q. For how long are Native Americans believed to have been living in Delaware?

A. At least twelve thousand years.

Q. State foresters believe that the largest tree in Delaware, a cypress with a circumference of twenty-five feet, is near what state park in Sussex County?

A. Trap Pond.

Q. From 1833 to 1846, what northern Delaware-based firm hunted large sea mammals?

A. Wilmington Whaling Company.

Q. Which Newark-based organization conducts physics and astronomical studies worldwide?

A. Bartol Research Foundation.

Q. When is the best time for dolphin-watching cruises at Delaware beaches?

A. July to October.

Q. In the 1800s what Wilmington firm was the largest U.S. maker of railroad wheels?

A. Lobdell Car Wheel Company.

Q. What Harvard astronomer from Delaware made a star catalog in the 1920s?

A. Annie Jump Cannon.

Q. What device is used by University of Delaware oceanographers to study the effects of sea conditions?

A. Tilting wind-wave-current tank.

Q. A 1998 aerial survey of snow geese showed how many of the birds in Delaware?

A. 280,000.

Q. How many gallons of water does Wilmington's Edgar M. Hoopes Reservoir hold?

A. Two billion.

Q. For what invention did Delaware's Oliver Evans gain fame in the nineteenth century?

A. Automated grain mills.

Q. What meteorological event in January 1992 damaged the Rehoboth Boardwalk?

A. Nor'easter.

Q. Ships traveling between Baltimore and Philadelphia can save how many miles by using the Chesapeake and Delaware Canal?

A. Around 285.

Q. Delaware's major electricity producer, Conectiv, was earlier known by what name?

A. Delmarva Power and Light Company.

Q. The U.S. Public Health Service once used Reedy Island in the Delaware River for what purpose?

A. Quarantine station.

Q. Which avian species including pintails and green-winged teals numbered 138,000 in a 1998 survey?

A. Ducks.

Q. What ingredients did the early du Ponts use to make their superior gunpowder?

A. Saltpeter, charcoal, and sulfur.

Q. What flourishing Yorklyn industry in the nineteenth century gave its name to an area road?

A. Snuff milling.

Q. How many "Recycle Delaware" recycling centers are there in the state?

A. Approximately one hundred.

———⊶⊷———

Q. What veterans' organization operated an ambulance service in the Smyrna area?

A. The American Legion.

———⊶⊷———

Q. Lower New Castle County residents get their water from what source?

A. Wells.

———⊶⊷———

Q. How many years can a Delaware Bay horseshoe crab live?

A. Thirty.

———⊶⊷———

Q. What airline was founded by World War II hero Richard C. DuPont as an aerial mail service?

A. USAirways.

———⊶⊷———

Q. What public gathering place in Wilmington contains an infrared network that helps amplify sound for the hard of hearing?

A. The Playhouse.

Q. The Delaware Aerospace Education program sponsors what spectacular event for schoolchildren each spring at Cape Henlopen?

A. Rocket launch.

———⊛———

Q. In 1987 what DuPont Company scientist won the prestigious Nobel Prize for chemistry?

A. Dr. Charles J. Pedersen.

———⊛———

Q. The layers of large stone that line Delaware's canals and other waterways are known technically by what name?

A. Riprap.

———⊛———

Q. What artistic outdoor attraction draws visitors and students to the University of Delaware's Goodstay Conference Center in Wilmington?

A. Tudor Gardens.

———⊛———

Q. For health reasons, shellfish may not be taken from the Delaware River shoreline north of what wildlife area?

A. Bombay Hook.

———⊛———

Q. What towering relics of World War II on the Christina River are reminders of Wilmington's industrial history?

A. Shipyard cranes.

Q. The Port of Wilmington is the top North American port of arrival for what sea-borne commodities?

A. Fresh fruit and produce.

———⊶⊷———

Q. What was the Richter-Scale magnitude of the most severe earthquake formally logged in Delaware, on February 28, 1973?

A. 3.8.

———⊶⊷———

Q. What is the name of the commuter airline that began scheduled passenger service from New Castle County Airport in 1998?

A. Shuttle America.

———⊶⊷———

Q. How many tons of steel were imported through the Port of Wilmington in fiscal year 1998?

A. 247,000.

———⊶⊷———

Q. When a 1999 Dodge Durango left the DaimlerChrysler assembly line in Newark, it was the what millionth car produced at the plant since 1957?

A. Seven.

———⊶⊷———

Q. What were the largest ships manufactured along the Christina River during World War II?

A. Four-hundred-foot cargo ships.

Q. The DuPont Co. uses what brand name for its three-layer polymer material used for vandal-proof, super-strong auto windows?

A. SentryGlas.

Q. The independent high school that concentrates on a math and science curriculum has what name?

A. Charter School of Wilmington.

Q. Which international company, with North American headquarters in Wilmington, developed tamoxifen, said to lower the risk of breast cancer?

A. Zeneca.

Q. The Brandywine River that passes through Wilmington may have gotten its name from what seventeenth-century streamside landowner?

A. Andrew Brandwyn.